SO-AXM-073

grassroots
evangelism

grassroots evangelism

DON MALLOUGH

BAKER BOOK HOUSE

Grand Rapids, Michigan 49506

Copyright © 1971 by Baker Book House Company
Grand Rapids, Michigan 49506

ISBN: 0-8010-5880-5

Library of Congress Card Catalog Number 72-172299

Printed in the United States of America

Prologue

EVANGELISM is to the work of the church what harvesting is to farming. Unless there is an ingathering, the labors of fertilizing, tilling the soil, sowing the seed, and cultivating become meaningless and vain. The culmination of all agricultural endeavors comes with the harvest. Likewise, the climax of all that is done in the name of Christ occurs in the winning of souls to the Saviour. Such evangelism is the very life throb of the church and without it decay and death ensue.

The title of this book was carefully chosen to graphically indicate its contents. The definition of grassroots is expressed as "originating among or carried on by the common people." In the early church, the burden of evangelism rested upon the rank and file, not only upon the leaders. The plan of God has never changed, although men have shifted the burden to the ministers in many periods of history — including the day in which we live. Alert Bible students are well aware of the folly of limiting evangelism to pulpit ministry. They are continually striving to put it back on its broad base where every individual has the responsibility to win

5

souls. The purpose of this book is to help in that cause.

Logic itself calls for every Christian to be a soul winner. If the harvest is ripe and time is of the essence, then the more individuals enlisted as harvesters, the more thorough will be the coverage of the harvest field. The urgency of the task demands that every Christian be challenged to win others to the Lord. In order to work effectively in His vineyard, the workers need instructions and suggested methods of procedure. This volume presents just such ideas and is produced to help Christians not only to start the task but also to continue it effectively.

By reading a book of this nature, an individual can be challenged to undertake the work of personal soul winning. Many such books have been written and many persons have been stirred to work more effectively in leading others to the fold. Even greater results will follow when groups or classes are inspired to fan out through a community in the work of witnessing. Many who would not respond to just the message of a book will get the burden of personal evangelism when in a class with others of like mind and purpose.

With that thought in mind, this volume is written to be used as a textbook in classes for personal evangelism. Not that a person cannot or will not read it for personal challenge. The basic thought is that more results will follow if classes are organized, experiences are shared, those gifted in witnessing set an example for the timid, and there be a body to which successful endeavors can be reported.

6

Classes can be formed among the men, the women, the young people, or any other group or classification. The subject can be studied in the midweek service, in the Sunday school, or in a personal evangelism conference. Through the medium of classes, many who would otherwise be reluctant even to start will be encouraged to launch out into personal witnessing.

Because we learn by doing, as well as by studying, some suggestions are given at the end of each chapter. Ideas are presented for mixing the practical with the theoretical, thus fostering a healthy balance. Such ventures make the class approach so much better than merely appealing to the individual. A basic rule for having a person carry out an assignment is also to give him a time and place to report back the results. The class is a logical place for that report.

No suggestion is made as to how fast the material of this book should be covered. Much will depend upon how many practical assignments are interwoven with the study and how thoroughly the teacher delves into given areas.

Before starting the class in personal work, the teacher should not only familiarize himself with the contents of this volume but also thoroughly read the suggestions to the instructor.

Every true Christian desires to be a soul winner. May the contents of this book help many to fulfill that desire.

Don Mallough

Suggestions to the Instructor

WHETHER or not the class in personal evangelism is a success depends much upon you, the teacher. *What* is taught is important, but *how* it is taught is far more so than many of us realize. If the objective in teaching is just to declare certain truths, then there need be little thought as to how those truths are presented. On the contrary, if the aim is to move the hearers to action and bring about tangible results, then careful planning should precede the class session and thus insure the best method of presentation.

It has already been called to your attention that class study has advantages over individual study. Experience in our educational system has proved that some persons will pursue studies on their own but most need the prodding of a teacher and the challenge and incentive offered in a classroom. When others are coping with the same problems, embracing the same facts, and receiving the same challenge, it inspires us to work better and the results will be greater. Particularly is that true when dealing with such a subject as personal evangelism. It calls for the work of witnessing in the work-a-day world, and an exchange of experience can be of greater inspiration than even the presentation of sound biblical truths. Because of that, a mingling of the practical with the theoretical is vital in such a subject as this.

At the end of each chapter in this book you will find one or more assignments. They are not lengthy but are very important. They are not to be viewed as something just tagged on. Neither are they there just to be read. They are planned assignments calculated to weave the practical in with the theoretical and give a well-rounded experience in soul winning. You may use them verbatim or you may adapt them or even substitute practical ones of your own. The important matter is to have assignments in memory work or practical activities following each session. You may overlook these in the book but if you don't use them, use something better. Give the class members some homework to do and they will progress faster.

Assignments are of no value unless the pupils are given opportunity to report on them. These that are suggested do not call for something in writing but there should be a chance to report orally on attempts and experiences. You may not be able to hear all of them, but every person should be alerted that he is subject to call for memory work or to tell of his practical efforts. That alert, in itself, is an incentive to do a good job. Such reports should not be counted as secondary to the teaching or anything else. With each experience he is allowed to report on, a person becomes the more bold, not only in doing personal work, but in telling about it. Encourage your students to exercise initiative in finding places to witness and how to do it. The timid person takes new heart to venture forth and is helped in that way. You can err easier in having too few of these sharing sessions than in allowing too much time for them.

You will notice that the assignments are related to the contents of the chapter. The farther the study progresses, the more responsibility the class member is given. In that way he grows in experience as well as in knowledge. If it is deemed wise to give special individual assignments, do so with the thought of using the talents of a given person for the inspiration of the entire class.

It would be very wise if, prior to every class session, you would spend some time planning *how* you are going to present the lesson. That would take in the teaching, of course, and the practical aspects and assignments as well. If there are two or three people with whom you could consult, that would be even better. For every soul winner you develop in your class, there will be multiplied souls brought into the possession of eternal life. Because of that, your work is of great importance and calls for thorough planning.

Anytime after studying chapter five, you will want to emphasize the use and memorization of the Scriptures. Sometimes interest in memory work can be created by making it somewhat of a game. Even a bit of competition in committing verses to memory adds zest to it. It may be that at a most unexpected time you can ask an individual in the class a question that will call for a scriptural answer. For instance, "You say I am a sinner; can you give me proof of it?" After studying chapters eight and nine you could ask any question for which they should have an answer in an exact quotation from the Bible. Effective teaching is more than lecturing. It embodies many tactics which create interest and elicit a response from those in the class.

Because chapter five makes a definite challenge for an immediate start in actual soul winning, that would be a good place to make a break and bring in some more of the practical. For the following class session, it might be good to have a change of pace and call it Scatter Night. Forget the textbook for that night but meet at the usual time and in the same place. Have an inspirational challenge to win souls and then send the group out, two by two, to do personal witnessing in various parts of the city. Some may go to parks, the airport, homes, hotel lobbies, or anywhere people are apt to congregate. If it would help them in making contacts to have a small tract to hand out, then provide some. However, it should not be merely a time of promiscuously distributing tracts. The tract should be but a means to the actual work of witnessing to one or more persons.

Sending out the witnesses two by two follows the example of our Lord. If it is practical, it would help to assign the partners rather than let them choose their own. A bold person or an experienced soul winner should be teamed up with a novice or one that is apt to be timid. That will help each of them to understand the other and they will both be better workers because of it.

Give a time limit for the witnessing, possibly one hour. Before the class disperses, set a definite time to meet back at the classroom. When all have returned, have a report session and allow time for each team to give an account of what they did. It might be helpful to have the timid one of the two give the report. Then you could end with a prayer session, remembering those who were contacted during that hour. It may be that after the first experience with a Scatter Night you will want to do it on other occasions.

At any time after the class has digested the material in chapter eight have them break up in teams of two with one person posing as the prospect and the other as the witness. Let the prospect give the excuses for not accepting Christ and the witness refute them with the Word of the Lord.

During the study you may want to suggest that the class participate in a project where each person will mark his New Testament, marking the key verses used in personal work. That, like other things, can be done by individuals but they are more apt to do it when a group is working together. The class can agree on various colors for different subjects. Testaments that are already marked are available but a person will learn more and cherish his Testament if he has marked it himself.

Much of what you can do during this study will be determined by how much time is spent on the course. The best results will come when the most time is available. If it is practical and possible, lead the class in going back over the material and reviewing it periodically.

It may be that this personal evangelism course can form the nucleus of a select group or club within the church or other sponsoring organization. Not that it need be an organization, itself, or have officers, etc. It could be a periodic meeting of those who are vitally interested in the same subject — soul winning. There need not be continued study on this subject, but a review now and then would be helpful and an inspirational challenge would give new impetus to the cause of personal work from time to time. The biggest value would be a mutual exchange of ideas and experiences. It could be a testimony meeting telling of the Lord's blessing in individual soul winning. Perhaps the group could meet once a month to share experiences. Because Andrew was basically a personal worker, it would be meaningful if the group would bear his name in some way. Perhaps it could be the Andrew Club, Associates of Andrew, Andrew's Partners, or just the Personal Evangelism Class. What you call the group is not as important as the work that it does in winning individuals to the Saviour.

There is only one thing better than soul winning — training many to become soul winners. To do that effectively you must be a soul winner yourself. As you whet the desire of others to be witnesses and mold them so they can serve the Lord in that capacity, you are fulfilling heaven's high purpose.

The calling of a teacher is a high one. Being a personal evangelist is a noble work. You have combined the two and thus are serving in a most responsible position. The blessing of God will surely be upon your efforts for His glory.

Contents

1. Focus on the Individual

BOTH the gospel and the principles of democracy are based upon the intrinsic value of the individual. It is when the view of the individual is obscured that we lose perspective and miss the target. And yet how easy it is to see a congregation instead of two hundred souls, to deal with America instead of Americans, and to study aggregate statistics instead of personal needs. Every person in public life, and most assuredly every Christian, could well have on his wall a constant reminder in the form of a motto, saying, "The Individual Is Important."

A classic example of a wrong perspective was told by Julia Ward Howe. She wrote a letter to a United States Senator in behalf of a man who was suffering a grave injustice. His curt reply was, "I am so much taken up with plans for the benefit of the human race that I do not have time for individuals." That a governmental leader should have such a viewpoint is bad, but it is much worse for a person to be so involved in bringing God's truth to the masses or the nations that he overlooks individual souls.

God does not deal with men collectively, but individually. Nations do not turn to God, and neither do cities. It is only as the majority of the citizens make a commitment to the Saviour that there are trends toward righteousness. People are not saved in lots of one hundred, fifty, or even ten. If, at the time of invitation, they step forth in such numbers, they come as that number of persons and respond as individuals to the summons of a personal Saviour.

Lord Eustace Percy grasped a truth that many leaders have never comprehended. He expressed it bluntly by saying, "He who sets out to change human lives may be an optimist; but he who sets out to change society without first changing the individual is a lunatic."

In our eagerness and haste to make converts, we overlook a basic premise of God's plan. We live in an age of technological progress and production-line methods. If that works in other realms, then why not in gospel work? Dealing with individuals seems slow and laborious. Hand-picked fruit is good, but it takes so long to get much of it. Is there not a way to save labor and multiply the results many times?

Such reasoning has produced the mass approach. Through the media of huge auditoriums, public address systems, tents, the printed page, and the miracles of radio and television, one man can appeal to multiplied thousands of people. Everything is done in a big style and in gigantic proportions. The individual becomes less and less important. Replacing him are crowds, listeners, viewers, readers, or cold statistics. Our motive is absolutely right — to win to Christ as many as we can in the least possible time — but in our eagerness we have seen only one way of accomplishing that and, thus, have overlooked the individual and made him only a digit in a gigantic total.

The common procedure is to use every available means to let one man, the preacher, reach the most people for Christ. There is another plan, too often overlooked, that will reach the masses and still preserve the personal touch. In it the individual plays an important role, both as the *messenger* of the gospel and as a *recipient* of the gospel. This method need not take second place to any other in results, yet it still emphasizes the value of the lowliest person and utilizes his talents. The quality of hand-picked fruit is preserved and the quantity of the production line is equaled or surpassed.

The principle is simple. Instead of devising ways for one person to reach greater throngs, challenge more people to reach individuals. Rather than allowing one person to have the joy of winning a thousand souls, let one thousand people get the taste of winning one soul each. When such a surge of accomplishment comes, eagerness to work for God will blossom like a flower. Such a plan of personal work is sound and is based on the principles of scriptural health and strength. The more participants there are in the soul-winning plan, the better it is. Even if the results were the same, the grass-roots approach to evangelism far surpasses any other. When given just a little time, it will go beyond other plans in results and in every other way.

A bishop in India once said, "Let me suppose that when Christ was on the earth He had come to our country. Let's say He ministered in one village each day and then moved on to another. If He had remained on earth from that day until now and preached in a different town every day, He still would not have covered all the towns of India alone — to say nothing of the world."

Such a statement is amazing to those who know not the teeming masses of India. It graphically shows the limitations of one man, even if He be the Lord Jesus Christ.

By way of contrast, it is interesting to ask yourself one question. "If every Christian in the world won another to the Lord each day, how long would it take until every living soul was a Christian?" The answer is surprising. Even when figured on the basic minimum of Christians, the task would be completed in less than a month. Do a little figuring and be convinced.

The Scriptures do not intimate that every person in the world will turn to Christ, but the contrast between one man's efforts and the potential with every disciple a soul winner veritably staggers the imagination.

Grassroots evangelism, that which originates among and is carried on by the common people, is not a new or an untried method. It is and always has been the basis of all evangelism. Periodically we must remind ourselves of its importance and return to it in common practice. The idea of using all Christians to reach all unbelievers far surpasses any other method of getting out the gospel or winning souls. There are five logical reasons why it will get the job done and why it surpasses any other method of evangelism.

1. IT IS BIBLICAL

If there were no other reason for challenging every Christian to be an aggressive soul winner, this would be sufficient. Jesus, Himself, set the example by dealing personally with Nicodemus (John 3), with the Samaritan woman (John 4), and with the impotent man (John 5). He dealt personally with at least sixteen other people. Andrew gives a noble demonstration of successful soul winning in leading his brother Peter to the Lord (John 1:40-42). Actually, seven out of eleven disciples were won through such personal work and, although details are not given, it may be that some of the others were also won that way. On the day of Pentecost, individuals noised abroad what had been happening. Private preaching culminated in public preaching. Those who were filled with the Holy Spirit began witnessing. The great sermon preached by Peter followed the concerted testimony of the believers. That set a great example for all the church as to correct procedure. Individual witnessing brought people to hear the sermon.

Our Lord sent forth some seventy believers, two by two, and thus started them off on their task of witnessing (Luke 10:1-11). Philip dealt with a single Ethiopian and was successful (Acts 8:25-39). Paul won both Lydia and a jailor; and he was willing to spend time with a preacher, Apollos, to lead him into a fuller understanding of the plan of God (Acts 18:24-28). He also used the method of going from door to door (Acts 20:20). One of the reasons for the phenomenal growth of the early church is that, as the people were scattered by persecution, they diligently witnessed and testified to those with whom they came in contact (Acts 8:4; 11:19). The history of the apostolic church is replete with examples of saved persons doing their part in soul winning.

2. IT ENGAGES MORE PEOPLE

Very often it is said, "The test of a leader is not what he can do himself but what he can inspire other men to do." It is axiomatic that the more people who are working for a given cause, the more interest there will be in it, and the better the results. The rut of complacency into which the church drifts when it leaves the soul winning to the ministers is basically wrong, if for no other reason than that it restricts the number of workers. The more people engaged in a task, the less the handicap when one person falters. The more people working, the greater the interest will be. The more numerous the witnesses, the greater the number of converts. Because it challenges all the believers, the program of personal evangelism is a good one.

3. IT CAN BE DONE ANY TIME OR ANY PLACE

Some situations and certain hours are not the most appropriate for a formal preaching service. That cannot be said of personal witnessing for Christ. At any time when two or more people are together, a fitly spoken word for the Lord is appropriate. It may be in a life raft on a storm-tossed sea; at lunchtime in a mine hundreds of feet underground;

as the plow furrows meet in the field; or at the toll gate on the turnpike. If souls could be saved only through hearing preaching, many are doomed to be lost. They are not interested in church, preaching, or the trappings of organized religion. The only way to penetrate their armored resistance is to wait for the right opportunity to witness and then deftly aim the right words into the chinks of their armor. Because personal witnessing can be done anywhere or at any time, it has an advantage over other methods of evangelism.

4. It reaches all classes of people

We must recognize that there are various classes of human beings. That does not necessarily mean one is more important in God's eyes than the other. Still there are divergencies of types of humans. The genteel and cultured gentleman is not apt to be interested in the testimony of the hard working sand hog who works in the tunnels under a teeming metropolis. The college professor is not going to be greatly interested in the religious experience of the illiterate who has just scratched an "X," in lieu of his name, on an application for welfare help. The minister who has always lived a sheltered life will not have the influence upon a gangster that a rough-spoken former companion would have.

There are people in our churches from all walks of life who have been saved. No matter how many strata of society there are, how many jargons are spoken, or what varied experiences men have had in the past, there is someone from the same background to tell how Christ saved and satisfies him. With every member an active soul winner, any class of person can be reached for the Saviour.

5. IT PRODUCES GREAT RESULTS

No matter how you figure or reason it, two hundred fervent witnesses can win more souls for Christ than one can — even though the one have the sounding board of a pulpit. Whatever reasons can be cited for not utilizing a program of every-member evangelism in our churches, it can never be said that the plan will not produce. Reasoning, common sense, the Scriptures, and experience all say that getting *all* the believers to win *all* the sinners is the ideal for producing eternal results.

Every human life is important and the soul of every person is exceedingly precious. The personal touch is important in human relations, in education, in politics, and in affairs between nations. How much more vital is that personal touch in matters spiritual. The pastor of a large church strives to keep contact with all his people and with new prospects. If he has assistants, they can help him. How happy he is when the members of the church become avidly interested in winning souls. When his congregation develops into a dynamo of witnessing power, his preaching is augmented by a host of helpers, dedicated to a work that God intended them to do. He sets the example to them and guides their endeavors. Instead of being only a voice trumpeting truths from a pulpit, he becomes the general of an army of soul winners. When a church attains that goal, it has fully accepted God's challenge and is utilizing all its power as a soul-saving center.

In a catastrophic mine disaster, those on the surface do not depend only on one with a loud voice to shout instructions down the shaft to the trapped. Volunteers are put to work in every way to do the practical tasks needed. Organized rescue operations use as many men as possible, and they work feverishly, prodded on by the value of the lives below.

When fire trucks converge on a burning building, the fire chief may shout instructions to those trapped on the top floor, but action is not limited to his advice. Men from various fire stations put up ladders, spread nets, operate hoses, and work diligently to save both lives and building.

It takes more than radioed instructions to help those on board a ship that is being battered on coastal rocks. Then is the time for practical help — to throw a line, to man rescue boats, or to set up a breeches buoy. Good instructions are a part, but only a part, of what is to be done at such a time.

Unified, practical efforts are just as needed in snatching souls from destruction as they are in any other rescue operation.

We have no thought of minimizing the preaching ministry, but only of showing the limitations of depending upon preaching alone. God never intended that the gospel should be proclaimed only by those who stand behind the sacred desk. Neither has He purposed that a minister should win souls in only that way. When evangelism becomes the burning passion of the pew as well as the pulpit, then the church will make rapid strides forward and be conscious of complying fully with the Great Commission.

Very often our sense of importance becomes distorted. We talk of the masses, aggregate attendance, and astounding statistics and surmise that importance and success are attached only to such collective accomplishments. We overlook the fact that two of the greatest sermons Jesus ever preached were to individuals: Nicodemus and the Samaritan woman. No apostolic leader was above dealing with one person. No great soul winner of the past, worthy of the name, dealt only with crowds or was too busy to talk to a needy soul. Henry Ward Beecher clinched the truth when he said, "The longer I live the more confidence I have in those sermons preached where one man is the congregation; where one man is the minister; and where there is not a question as to who is meant when the preacher says, 'Thou art the man.' "

Individuals are important. They can best be won to Christ by other individuals who have come from a similar walk of life and have been saved by grace. The work of the church is to put all the Christians of the world to work winning all the sinners of the world.

ASSIGNMENT

Make a list of five individuals you know who stand in need of salvation. Let them be those nearby, with whom you often come in contact. Put the list on your bedroom mirror or in some conspicuous place. Make it a point to pray for those persons by name two or three times a day.

2. A Mandate to Witness

EVERY CHILD OF GOD has been commissioned to be a soul winner. The ceremony took place in the great post-resurrection gathering at which the eleven disciples were present, and possibly the bulk of the five hundred brethren who had seen Jesus after His triumph over death. That commission was not limited to eleven or five hundred men. In no sense was it restricted to full-time ministers, apostles, or the first century church. Those present to hear the vibrant words from the lips of the Saviour were but depositories of the divine commands and were charged to transmit them to others. That commission has been passed down in uninterrupted succession, right to the present day.

The Great Commission was not given to the disciples, but to the church. It was not given exclusively to ministers, but to all believers. It proscribed the work of the church and gave the authority and source of power for winning souls. The task for making disciples is not limited to a certain segment of the church but is the principal work of all the church. The charge was not given to men who would witness consecutively in one place and then another. It was imparted to those who could be thus

27

witnessing simultaneously in various parts of the world.

Any person who has been born into the mystical body of the church has been ordained to be a soul winner. The words of Jesus ring out just as forcefully today as ever: "All power is given unto me in heaven and in earth. Go ye therefore, and teach all nations, baptizing them in the name of the Father, and of the Son, and of the Holy Ghost: Teaching them to observe all things whatsoever I have commanded you: and, lo, I am with you alway, even unto the end of the world" (Matthew 28:18-20).

The believer in Christ claims this mandate to witness as his very own. In the four *alls* of the declaration, he finds just what he needs to carry on the work of personal evangelism. *All power* is the source of strength; *all nations* presents the sphere of his operations; *all things* covers the scope of the message; and *always* gives the assurance of continued divine help in the task. The person who sees only his own weakness and inability need not tremble but can be bold in the face of *all power,* which is at his disposal. Because *all power* is given to Christ, *therefore* we are to launch forth as witnesses and know that He is with us. The prerogative of witnessing belongs to all the church — as does the responsibility to do so.

Another challenge to witness was given to us in the very last words of our Lord before His ascension. Last words are often significant and these were certainly so. Jesus told His disciples they were to tarry in Jerusalem until they be endued with power from on high. He foretold of a service that would be theirs and of an ever widening sphere of influence they could have in that witnessing. Hear His words: "But ye shall receive power, after that the Holy Ghost is come upon you: and ye shall be witnesses unto me both in Jerusalem, and in all Judea, and in Samaria, and unto the uttermost part of the earth" (Acts 1:8).

Again the promise was not only to disciples or ministers. On the day of Pentecost they were *all* filled with the Holy Ghost. It was when the Spirit of God came upon them that they were to become witnesses. The promise of the Holy Spirit is for all. "For the promise is unto you, . . . even as many as the Lord our God shall call" (Acts 2:39). No class , sex, disposition, age, or race can claim an exemption from that promise. If we are filled with the Holy Spirit, it is to make us witnesses for the Saviour. If we have not received the fullness of the Spirit, He desires that we be filled to accomplish His plan.

The mention of the word *witness* is the first of some thirty references to it in the Book of Acts. It plays an important part in the early history of the church. A witness is one who knows and is summoned to tell what he knows. Originally the word meant *martyr*. We think of a martyr as one who dies for his faith. Many a man died for his faith because he was a martyr or witness.

As all men receive the baptism of the Holy Spirit, they go forth in boldness to stand before all classes of men and speak of Jesus Christ. They bear witness like Nathan before David, like John before King Herod, like Paul before Felix, or with the boldness of Luther before kings and cardinals at Worms.

In the plan of God, every child of God has a ministry. Everything in the program of the church points toward the responsibility of all believers to bear their part of the mandate to witness.

It is unfortunate that the impact of such a truth is lessened and a statement obscured by the addition of a comma in one verse of our Authorized Version of the Bible. When the comma is dropped, the full force of God's plan is sensed. The portion that is clouded by the comma is Ephesians 4:11-12. It reads, "And he gave some, apostles; and some, prophets; and some, evangelists; and some, pastors and teachers; for the perfecting of the saints, for the work of the ministry, for the edifying of the body of Christ." The unnecessary comma follows the word *saints*. When the comma is deleted, the passage says, "for the perfecting of the saints for the work of the ministry." The ministry gifts and offices of the church are to perfect the church members for the ministry. Their ministry, task, and responsibility is that of witnessing and doing personal work. The leaders of the church are to devote their efforts to develop the believers for the great task of winning souls.

Many of the more recent translations of the New Testament more clearly bring out this great truth. Weymouth expresses it lucidly, saying, "And He Himself appointed some to be apostles, some to be prophets, some to be evangelists, some to be pastors and teachers, in order to fully equip His people for the work of serving."

One of the latest versions is the Amplified New Testament. It also clearly emphasizes this truth.

"His intention was the perfecting and the full equipping of the saints (His consecrated people), [that they should do] the work of ministering toward building up Christ's body (the church)."

The church is not to be a stagnant sea into which flows the truth of God from the lips of apostles, prophets, evangelists, pastors, and teachers. It is to be a fresh water reservoir which both receives and passes on to others. It is a Lake of Galilee instead of a Dead Sea. The consecrated people of the Lord are not only to receive but also, in return, to give in an outflowing ministry. This is the eternal plan of God that has often been diverted but never stopped. It is the program of grassroots evangelism and places the responsibility for soul winning on all those who bear the name of Christ.

Our Lord was not only aware of His own mission but also He likened our responsibility to His. He said, ". . . as my Father hath sent me, even so send I you" (John 20:21). On a previous occasion He had said, "For the Son of man is come to seek and to save that which was lost" (Luke 19:10). If His prime objective was to pursue the lost and bring salvation to them, then we have the same responsibility. The identical commission that was His is passed down to every believer. The early Christians were constantly reminded that they were witnesses (John 15:27; Acts 1:8; 1:22; 2:32; 3:15; 5:32; 10:39; 26:16). That charge was given to the disciples but did not end there. The apostle Paul urged Timothy to pass on the instruction to others. "And the things that thou hast heard of me among many witnesses, the same commit thou to faithful

31

men, who shall be able to teach others also" (II Timothy 2:2). It was the same message, privilege, and responsibility of winning the lost that was to be passed from one generation to another. In that way the torch has been handed to every one of us and it is now our task and privilege to be soul winners.

An exemplary experience for all Christians is that of the apostle Paul. He stated as much when he wrote, "Howbeit for this cause I obtained mercy, that in me first Jesus Christ might shew forth all longsuffering, for a pattern to them which should hereafter believe on him to life everlasting" (I Timothy 1:16). Paul (Saul of Tarsus) met the Saviour in a glorious experience on the Damascus road. After he had seen and heard Him, he was to be a witness of those things to all men. That is the God-ordained plan. After a person has had a vital experience with the Saviour, he is expected to be a witness of what has happened. After such a glorious event, who could refrain from telling about it? It is only natural for new converts to tell what the Lord has done for them. In general instances, it is in afteryears that many drift into smug complacency and relinquish to others the task that God wants them to do.

In the face of all this clear evidence of God's plan for every believer, why is there such a neglect of personal work? If the Bible is so plain, how can devout Christians be satisfied to let just a few carry the responsibility and get the joy of dealing with individuals about spiritual matters? In view of the clear message of the Word of God, they must have some very logical reasons for their attitude. If not reasons and not logical, then they must have excuses for neglecting this great part of God's plan. What are those excuses?

There are four basic excuses believers use for not exercising their privilege and responsibility to win individuals to the Saviour. In some instances they are only excuses and in others they seem to be reasonable. In no case are they so formidable that they won't disappear in the light of God's Word.

1. TIMIDITY AND FEAR

This is possibly the greatest hindrance to personal work. Some people are exceedingly shy and suffer paroxysms of fear at the mere thought of approaching a total stranger, or even a friend, about spiritual things. Those people are in the minority. Strangely, some individuals are extroverts in speaking about anything but the truth of Christ. They have a glib tongue in business, on social occasions, or even in public speaking but would have themselves believe that they are afraid to witness for Christ. Often in seeking a justification for their laxity, they have developed a fear psychosis and it becomes a plague of their own making. It is an artificial impasse, but to them very real.

Whether the fear is innate or artificial, it is not necessary for it to dominate any life. To say that it must is to ascribe it a power greater than that of Christ. The one who gave us a commission to witness for Him also said, "All power is given unto me." To those who want Him to be, He is greater than any fear psychosis. It is He who "baptizeth with the Holy Ghost" and thus gives unto us the power to *witness* and the power for *service*.

Fear is often real, but in no instance is it greater than God. The wise man said, "The fear of man bringeth a snare: but whoso putteth his trust in the Lord shall be safe" (Proverbs 29:25).

2. LACK OF KNOWLEDGE

With few exceptions, every Christian feels he is limited in his knowledge of the Bible. Many sense such a lack and confess that they are not conversant enough with the Good Book to quote it with ease. Particularly do they feel their inferiority when dealing with one who might contradict or attempt to argue.

Even this can be an excuse instead of a reason for not witnessing. First of all, it does not take a profound understanding of the Bible to lead a soul to Christ. If one were to study the Bible all his life, he would still hesitate the first time he made an attempt to do personal work. One can learn more in a feeble effort at witnessing than in a full college course of study.

If there is an actual lack of basic knowledge for soul winning, it can be acquired hurriedly — provided there is an earnest desire. Books, such as this one, and special classes are at the fingertip of any individual. If lack of knowledge is only an excuse, it will remain so until the attitude of the person is changed.

3. SHIFTING THE RESPONSIBILITY TO OTHERS

An artificial barrier has been erected to divide two segments of the Christian church. In one airtight compartment are the ministers, and in the other the laymen. It is assumed that one is called by God and that the other is not. One has the privilege of working for the Lord and the other evaluates his position by saying, "I am only a layman." The supposed reason for the wall is that the work of one group is considered to be vastly different from the other and, hence, they should be segregated.

The barrier between these two groups is purely artificial, and yet it remains. The minister has a high calling, but so has the layman. Both are called to be soul winners.

An amateur at tennis plays the same game as the professional. He may have less time to devote to practice because he must earn a living from another source. He may not be as skilled as the one who has devoted his whole life to the game and receives remuneration from it. Still, both of them are tennis players. In like manner both the layman and the minister are to be soul winners and team up toward a common goal. The degree of ability is not pertinent.

It is common for the laymen to shift the responsibility for soul winning upon the shoulders of the ministers. Some are bold enough to suggest audibly that they contribute financially to enable the minister to win souls and that this is their only responsibility in the matter. Others do not say it but indicate as much by their attitude. A partial rationalizing of

35

that opinion is that the layman cannot do the job as well as the ministers, and so it is left to the latter. That idea is based on the false assumption that a minister has certain advantages in dealing with individuals in spiritual matters.

The truth is that the layman has advantages over the minister is doing personal work. When a clergyman broaches the subject of religion in a conversation, it is assumed he is doing so professionally. That is his business and he is talking about it because he is expected to. His remarks are accepted as those of an overly enthusiastic salesman or professional man talking shop. He is just expected to talk on that subject.

When the layman speaks about Christ, the men around him take notice. There is no professional reason for his witnessing; thus they pay attention, all the while wondering why he is saying such things.

The fact remains that both the layman and the minister are called to be soul winners. There is no hint in the Bible that their work should be different — only that one can devote his whole time to it. Hence, there is no justification for either group to shift to the other the responsibility for soul winning.

4. LACK OF CONCERN

A compassion for the lost will cause men to win souls. If a person senses fully the value of a soul — what it means to be eternally lost — and realizes that many people around him are in that condition, he will do something about it. If he is doing nothing to win his neighbor, it is a very good indication that he has little concern for that neighbor's soul.

An atheist was arguing with his neighbor, a Christian. He asked him if he believed in hell, a literal hell, and that every rejecter of Christ is going there. In answer to each question, the Christian gave an emphatic "Yes!"

"I don't believe any of those things," sneered the atheist. "But I'll tell you one thing. If I believed what you say you believe, I wouldn't be sitting around doing nothing. I'd be working night and day trying to save my friends and neighbors from such a fate."

A paragon of godly concern for the lost is found in Paul's words: ". . . I could wish that myself were accursed from Christ for my brethren, my kinsmen according to the flesh" (Romans 9:3); or in the prayer of Moses, ". . . and if not, blot me, I pray thee, out of thy book which thou hast written" (Exodus 32:32). Another noble example is the sight of Paul sitting in Athens until ". . . his spirit was stirred in him, when he saw the city wholly given to idolatry" (Acts 17:16).

A lack of concern is a reason for not being a soul winner, but it is doubtful if it is a justifiable one in the light of the Scriptures and the goodness of God to usward.

Whether they be reasons or excuses, the supposed justifications for not engaging in personal evangelism collapse like a paper bridge. It is clearly not a matter of whether God has *called* us to be soul winners, or whether we *should* be, but rather whether or not we *want* to be. If we are failing in such endeavors, the fault must be laid at our own doorstep. It is our complacency and indifference that is responsible for our idleness.

When our Lord called Peter, He used a very interesting word. He was comparing and contrasting his old vocation of fishing with that of his new work of winning souls. He said, ". . . from henceforth thou shalt catch men" (Luke 5:10). The Greek word for *catch* is an unusual one, *zogreo*. It has the full meaning of *to catch alive*. By the studied use of that word, Jesus was contrasting between catching fish and catching men. In the case of fish, they were taken from the water where they live to the air where they die. When you catch men, they are taken from death and into life. When exploring the similar features between the two vocations, there are also interesting facets. Archbishop Trench has given a picturesque comparison between the two:

"Those that were wandering, restless and at random, through the deep, unquiet waters of the world, the smaller falling prey to the greater, and all with a weary sense of a vast prison, he shall embrace if they break not through, nor leap over, they shall at length be drawn up to shore, out of the dark, gloomy waters into the bright, clear light of day, so that they may be gathered into vessels of eternal life."

The contrast between the great work of catching men for Christ and the trifling matters that take up so much of our time is most startling. A true evaluation of the difference will, of itself, stir us to do the work of personal soul winning. What we think to be so vastly important pales into insignificance in the presence of God's program — snatching men from the throes of death and bringing them into eternal life.

Soul winning is the greatest work and the heaviest responsibility that God could entrust to men. Solomon, who knew about God-given wisdom, said, "He that winneth souls is wise" (Proverbs 11:30). The Revised Version makes it read, "He that is wise winneth souls." That would indicate that the possession of wisdom precedes the winning of souls. It is not necessarily that the person is wise because he wins souls, but that he wins souls because he is wise.

Another man of God, Daniel, emphasized the wisdom of soul winning. "And they that be wise shall shine as the brightness of the firmament; and they that turn many to righteousness as the stars forever and ever" (Daniel 12:3). James stressed the importance of the work when he wrote, "Let him know, that he which converteth the sinner from the error of his way shall save a soul from death, and shall hide a multitude of sins" (James 5:20).

There is no greater joy than to be the instrument, under God, in leading a soul from darkness to light. It is a noble work, a satisfying work, and an eternal work. It is not only worthwhile but also delightful. Only those who have not tasted its joys find excuse to avoid it. Even greater than all other reasons for such effort is the promise that soul winners will hasten the coming of the Lord.

Every person who claims to be a Christian has a mandate to witness for Christ. Through prayer and witnessing, he must speak to God in behalf of sinners and speak to sinners in behalf of God.

ASSIGNMENT

Memorize Matthew 28:18-20 and Acts 1:8 and be able to quote them as the authority for your doing personal work. Do the same with John 20:21 and Luke 19:10 and as you couple them together you will have a greater sense of your call.

3. A Twofold Alert

TO BE A SUCCESSFUL SOUL WINNER, a person must sincerely want to win men to Christ. This entails more than mere idle wishing. If that were sufficient, then every professing Christian would be a soul winner. It also embraces more than just talking about winning souls to Christ, acknowledging the joys and potentials of such an effort, or resolving to do more along that line some day. There is no better time to begin than today and no substitute for starting — even if only falteringly.

The average person is acutely aware of his insufficiency, inability, and inadequacy in this realm. Even that sense of shortcoming is an asset rather than a liability. Such an individual can lean heavily upon the promise, "If any of you lack wisdom, let him ask of God, that giveth to all men liberally, and upbraideth not; and it shall be given him" (James 1:5). The person who senses his own weakness and lack will be the first to receive the abundant supply from the Lord. An example to us is in the record of Acts 4. The brethren of the early church prayed, "And now, Lord, . . . grant unto thy servants, that with all boldness they may speak thy word" (verse 29). The results of that prayer are recorded in verse 33: "And with great power gave the apostles witness of the resurrection of the Lord Jesus: and great grace was upon them all." What happened to them then can happen to any one of us today.

A basic trait in the life of all successful soul winners is alertness. Some come by this trait instinctively, and others develop it. The individual who wants to be used of God in doing personal work should do his utmost to develop the characteristic of being alert, as it is a point of beginning in making contacts. A person can know all the rules and be qualified to speak to anyone about spiritual matters and still do nothing, if he is not alert to hear the voice of the Spirit of God or quick to spot an opening to witness for the Lord. The need is for a twofold alertness that reaches both upward and outward. Because the Spirit of God can best direct us to needy souls, it is necessary that we hear and heed His voice. He may speak at any time and even in the faintest whisper. We must incline our ear to His voice. It is just as needful that we sense the opportunity to speak a fitting word for the Lord. That chance may come according to plan, or it may pop up at an unexpected moment. The wise soul winner will sense the appropriate time to speak of spiritual matters and know when to drive home the truth. The secret of alertness in soul winning is twofold, alert to the leadings of the Lord and alert to the opportunities to reach men.

The most vivid scriptural example of a soul winner being led of the Spirit of God is given in the eighth chapter of the Acts of the Apostles. An Ethiopian leader had been to a religious festival. He was hungry for spiritual knowledge but was going away with that yearning unsatisfied. In spite of his disappointment, he continued to read the Scriptures in search of truth, which was evidence of his sincerity. His chariot rolled along a desert road far from the religious throngs or anyone who could be of help to him. Seemingly his last chance for help had passed.

Quite some distance away, in the city of Samaria, was Philip, the only man who in the Scriptures is called an evangelist. He had gone to that city to preach. The people were unusually receptive to his message and a great revival broke out. It was an experience of a lifetime. Natural reasoning and observation would say he had found his niche and that he should remain there where God was using him so greatly. His personal desires concurred with that reasoning.

Here were two men, who, though miles apart, needed to get together. One had power to impart knowledge and the other had a disposition to receive it. One was a soul winner and the other was an honest, unprejudiced, teachable inquirer. What personal worker would not want to meet such a seeker? Even leaving a great revival to contact that type of person would be no sacrifice.

But how could getting these two together come about? In natural reasoning and planning it could never be done. Only God knew of the receptiveness of the Ethiopian to the gospel truth and the eagerness of Philip to do the Lord's bidding. The key to the whole situation was the alertness of Philip to receive and obey the sealed orders of the General of this great army, who sits on His throne in the heavens. Such communications brought together these two men who needed each other, even though so far apart in many ways: One of them was an Asiatic and the other an African. One was a commoner and the other an aristocrat. One was poor and the other rich. One was white and the other black.

The meeting of Philip and the eunuch was not the result of accident or chance. In the vocabulary of God there is no such word as chance. If a person is to be genuinely converted, he must be conditioned for that experience. No amount of human effort, persuasion, or reasoning can bring about the new birth in the life of an individual. Someone has said, "I can no more convert a soul than I can create a star." If it is God who makes possible the transformation known as conversion, then it is logical for Him to bring the human instrument into contact with the prospective Christian. Circumstances would say it was folly for Philip to seek the eunuch, but God's angel told him to do so. When the Spirit says to contact anyone, it is safe and profitable to do so.

It is not foreign to the Christian faith to suppose that God can lead us in matters of this nature. The history of the early church in the Book of Acts is profuse with instances of such leadings, sometimes in matters that seem almost trivial to us. An angel appeared to Cornelius with instructions as to what he should do to contact the man of God and be taught in the way of salvation (Acts 10:1-7). The Spirit of God also spoke to Peter so that he too would be prepared. When the apostles were delivered by an angel, they received instructions from the heavenly

44

being as to what they were to do (Acts 5:19-20). In a similar way an angel gave instructions to Peter when he was delivered from prison (Acts 12:7-8). When Paul and others were in dire peril, an angel brought him a message of consolation and assurance (Acts 27:23-25). Those who are prone to doubt the leadings of the Spirit would find the sixteenth chapter of Acts informative: Paul thought it not strange to be forbidden of the Holy Ghost to preach the Word in Asia (verse 6). He later wanted to go into Bithynia but the Spirit did not allow him to do so (verse 7). He had an unusual vision calling him to Macedonia (verse 9). After Peter had seen his vision on the housetop, ". . . the Spirit said unto him, Behold three men seek thee" (Acts 10:19). He was then given instructions as to just what he was to do. All of these experiences were leadings of the Lord and were a part of God's plan.

Even in this day, God can whisper in the ear of His servant and cause him to hurry to an earnest, seeking soul. It may not be an angel nor an audible voice, but it can be a clearcut witness of the Holy Spirit. The personal worker who depends on God to lead him in his contacts and is sensitive to the movings of the Holy Spirit will find his work fruitful and blessed. A successful soul winner must be alert to the voice of God. He will not only lead him to the person but will also suggest the course of action, as He did for Philip.

Although alertness for opportunities to witness is basically our responsibility, we are dependent upon the Lord in this also. At the beginning of any day or activity the soul winner should ask God for an

45

alertness to speak to the proper person under the proper circumstances. Certainly he won't button-hole every person he meets and speak to him about the Lord. Neither will the witnessing be done in a hit-or-miss style. Using innate wisdom, which in itself is God-given, and depending upon the guidance of the Lord, every contact can be made to count.

It is wise to anticipate contacts well before they transpire. Successful business and professional men spend some time each morning reviewing the plans for the day and refreshing their memory as to what they can expect or whom they are scheduled to see. Then if preparation is needed for certain appointments, it can be made. Those who count soul winning as important can take a leaf out of the book of the businessman and do likewise.

The systematic person will take a moment to make a list of the people he expects to see during the day. The list won't include those who regularly cross his path or those to whom he has often spoken about eternal truths. It will not include those who are sincere Christians. It will be a prospect list for witnessing, just as an insurance salesman has a prospect list. Which one would be the most receptive? How could spiritual truths be injected into an anticipated conversation? What is the wisest approach to this person? Any planned approach is better than an impromptu one. If there is no time or opportunity to make a written list, then he should make a mental one. Such a list can be made while commuting, while waiting for an appointment, or anticipating a visitor. As this plan is practiced, amazing opportunities will come to the fore. Start in a simple way and let the plan develop as you go along.

Our mental attitude generally determines what we will see. Three men can ride along in the same car. The farmer will observe the crops, the county commissioner will see the condition of the road, and the implement salesman will see the rickety tractor in the field and its owner as a prospect for a sale. If the most important pursuit is business customers, then we will find them. If we are searching for recreational outlets, then important landmarks will be woods, lakes, and streams. If the main objective of the day's work is a sum of money, then our eyes will be peeled for sales, percentages, and profits. The object we are looking for most is what we will likely find. If the day is started with a sincere desire to witness for Christ, natural law and the Spirit of God will work toward the developing of that opportunity. You can count on its coming.

There are certain contacts for which no plans can be made. Those are the people you meet unexpectedly and with whom you have but a few words. If the conversation is to turn to the things of Christ, it must of necessity be impromptu. It is at such a time that a brief word will give an opening. Even a casual question such as, "What have you been doing?" brings an opportunity to mention spiritual matters in an inoffensive way. The person looking for an opportunity to witness will find it even in such casual conversations.

Personal evangelism need not be a high pressure process. Actually, it is anything but that. The key is in speaking the right word at the right time.

When properly done, there is no need for foot-in-the-door tactics or the clobbering of the prospect with arguments. The principles of salesmanship are used, but not the high pressure that leaves the prospect hardly able to catch his breath — much less think.

Although there is no need for overpowering the prospect, the soul winner can look for opportunities that will place him in an advantageous position. Personal work can be done at any time, from any position, or under any circumstances. In spite of that fact, there are occasions and situations which are advantageous to the soul winner; and, insofar as possible, he should seek out such spots.

A sleek, shiny automobile stops along the highway to pick up a hitchhiker. The driver and the lad start a conversation. If one of them is an alert soul winner and wants to bear witness for Christ, will he be at advantage or disadvantage? If the driver is the soul winner he will have the advantage. The car is his and the young man is riding along at his invitation and through his kindness. The hitchhiker is already indebted to him and, hence, will be more apt to listen. If the rider were the soul winner, it would be a bit more difficult although it has been done many times. (Philip was actually a guest in the chariot of the Ethiopian, but he was successful in his efforts.)

If a car salesman is in process of closing a deal and the customer says, "Now just before I sign this, will you be so kind as to let me take three minutes to tell you about Someone who is very dear to me?" that man will listen at such a time, if he never would before. In such a case the customer has an advantage and knows it. He uses it as a time to speak of Christ.

A standard practice among salesmen is to invite a prospect to a steak dinner. At the time of the invitation, the guest may not even know he is a prospect. After an enjoyable social time a casual question is asked: "In the light of spiraling costs, have you considered increasing your insurance protection?" Suddenly the boom is lowered and the plan of the salesman is immediately apparent. This was not a sporadic invitation born of friendship alone. It was planned with the thought of asking a key question at a time when the prospect was indebted to the host. The salesman not only planned the contact but did so in such a way that he would be in an advantageous position when the question was asked.

Opportunities to witness for Christ abound on every hand but only the alert see them. If we are looking for them we will find them. If we plan for such opportunities we will make them develop. Taking our cue from the salesman, we will study the opportunities, put ourselves in their pathway, time things so that we will be at advantage, and close the deal at the earliest possible moment.

Who among us has invited a friend or a couple (not large groups) to dinner, with the paramount object of witnessing for Christ? Who has made a list of the firms he patronizes most and planned to witness to the personnel with whom he deals? (The customer has the advantage there.) Who has thought about his subordinates and associates and purposed that he would at least talk to them about the secular? Such a person is alert to the possibilities of soul winning and is making his experience with God the more real by sharing it with others.

A good rule of thumb for a soul winner is:

> Listen for promptings.
> Pray for opportunities.
> Plan for witnessing.

ASSIGNMENT

Between now and the next class session, be alert for possibilities to witness and keep a record of your attempts. In the morning make a list of those to whom you would like to bear witness. For the present, don't worry about the follow-through. Be content to say just a word for the Lord. Record your failures as well as your successes and analyze the reasons for them. Be prepared to report on the outstanding ones at the next class session.

4. Ply the Sword!

THE BIBLE is the master tool of the soul winner. It is the trumpet of the watchman, the trowel of the mason, the hammer of the carpenter, and the sword of the warrior. It alone shows the way of salvation (II Timothy 3:15) and presents the one who is the exclusive door to eternal life (John 10:9). By it, flinty hearts are softened, the defenses of the sinner are demolished, and terror comes to evildoers. The precepts of this greatest of all books turn the footsteps of the sinner into the paths of righteousness. So the Word of God should be in the hand of the soul winner, implanted in both his mind and heart and subject to an instant summons to his lips.

On several occasions the Word of God is called a sword. In the exhortation of the apostle Paul to don the whole armor of God he refers to "the sword of the Spirit, which is the word of God" (Ephesians 6:17). The Bible is called the sword of the Spirit because it was the Holy Spirit which brought it into existence and He also teaches us how to use the Word aright. It is also the instrument through which the Spirit works. The Scriptures are the Christian's weapon for both offense and defense in the battle against the forces of darkness. If you must be

51

caught on the battlefield without any one piece of armor or equipment, let it be anything but your sword — the Bible.

A graphic analogy of the Bible as a sword is given by the writer of Hebrews. "For the word of God is quick, and powerful, and sharper than any two-edged sword, piercing even to the dividing asunder of soul and spirit, and of the joints and marrow, and is a discerner of the thoughts and intents of the heart" (Hebrews 4:12). The words *quick and powerful* could well be translated *alive and active*. A sword with two edges has no blunt sides. It is pointed, bright, and keen. It is of tempered metal that does not break easily. It is incisive, penetrating, and piercing. With its thrust comes a probing into the innermost recesses of the being. It divides and severs the seemingly impenetrable and indistinguishable.

There are several ways in which the Bible and the sword of a warrior are much alike. From the references to that likeness, even within the Scriptures themselves, we are encouraged to recognize that similarity in more detail. There are four such basic likenesses.

1. THE SWORD IS A PRACTICAL WEAPON

It is utilitarian in that it is not only for decoration, but also for use. When sheathed in a scabbard it is of little practical value. It becomes an asset only when doing the task for which it was intended. Swords are used for dress parade as Bibles are used for display, but if that is the only use then the value is nil.

The swordsman keeps his weapon handy, uses it speedily and with skill in parrying and thrusting the enemy. It is as near as his right arm and as valuable. The active soul winner must have his Bible handy and use it readily, and he will find in it a weapon unsurpassed.

2. THE SWORD IS COMMON TO SOLDIERS OF ALL RANKS

Some implements of warfare are used only by a select few who are trained for that purpose. Others are beneath the dignity of some officers. The sword is available to and used by those in all echelons of the army. In like manner the Bible is the companion and weapon of both the minister, who has devoted his whole life to its study, and to the new convert who has a desire to win his friends to the Lord.

3. THE SWORD IS SUITED FOR MULTIPLE PURPOSES

Single purpose weapons are all right in specialized phases of warfare. They are useless in others. The sword is an all-around weapon for varied types of combat. Better always to have *it* at hand instead of an instrument that may or may not be useful in a given situation. Comments about the Bible, books that explain it, and helps at soul winning are fine; but it is better to have the old trusty Bible or Testament always available in order to be equipped for every situation that may arise.

4. THE SWORD MUST BE PLIED BY THE INDIVIDUAL

Gigantic cannons, depth bombs, antiaircraft guns, and such modern military equipment require unified efforts and cannot be operated by one man. There is a place for such weapons and their use. On the other hand, the sword is fashioned for the individual and used by him alone. The person who sets out to win others to the Lord has a personalized weapon in his Bible or Testament. With it, and the help of the Spirit of God, he cannot fail.

Every Christian has a Bible, but all do not have a small New Testament that can be carried on the person. Such Testaments, which are both small and thin, are available for a nominal sum. They can be carried in the shirt pocket, the breast pocket of a coat, or in a ladies pocketbook. The first step toward soul winning is to get such a Testament and the second is to get into the habit of carrying it. Before long it will be second nature to have it with you as surely as you have your keys, billfold, or driver's license. If by accident you forget it, you will feel undressed. We who do not carry a package of cigarettes certainly have room for something smaller than that and far more valuable — a Testament.

Once you are carrying the Scriptures on your person, don't be content with just that. Keep the sword polished and bright by constant usage. Remember, it is not a decoration nor a charm. During World War II, reports filtered through of instances where lives were spared because a Testament in a shirt pocket stopped a bullet that was almost spent. That led to some publishers putting steel covers on Testaments to be used by soldiers. The Bible is not meant to be that type of a shield. One cynic aptly pointed out that a deck of cards would have accomplished the same purpose.

Carry your Testament (in some instances the sight of it will open the door for witnessing) but also use it. Familiarize yourself with verses useful in winning souls. Utilize spare moments by reading the Word or memorizing texts. Mark the verses that are your favorites. The harder usage you give your Testament, the better. Another can be bought when you wear one out. God is not displeased with a worn Bible that is tattered from usage but with the beautifully bound and kept one that shows no sign of having been opened. Have a sword, carry it with you at all times, and use it.

When dealing with hungry souls, don't hesitate to read from or quote the Bible. Even if you can quote verbatim by memory, bring out the Testament anyway to give added emphasis and authority. Spurgeon and others have said, "It is not our comment on the Word that saves, but the Word itself." The Word of God will not return void, so let it go forth.

As a very young man I tried my prowess as a door-to-door salesman. The first time I was confronted by a metal sign on a doorstep saying, "No agents or peddlers, please," I cautiously backed away from that house. Veteran salesmen laughed heartily at my timidity. They said, "Those signs don't mean a thing. We sell more goods at those houses than at others." You may have a similar feeling when you are confronted by a person who says he doesn't believe the Word of God. Don't let that frighten you. It is still God's Word and will strike telling blows. Let it speak and it will do its job. The Lord describes the nature of His Word when He says, "Is not my word like as a fire? saith the Lord; and like a hammer that breaketh the rock in pieces?" (Jeremiah 23:29).

It is essential that the soul winner memorize certain portions of the Word of God. The process of concentrating and memorizing will itself be most profitable. Having scriptural truths stored away for instant recall is far better than the best filing system. The human memory is the greatest storehouse known, and the most helpful item that can be filed there is the Word of God. Then, if you do not have a Bible available, you still have its accurate message. It can be called to mind for your own consolation and encouragement or to present the truth to one who direly needs it.

We are repeatedly admonished to know the Word of God and to be able to quote it. Even the ancient people of God were told, ". . . thou shalt meditate therein day and night, that thou mayest observe to do according to all that is written therein: for then thou shalt make thy way prosperous, and then thou shalt have good success" (Joshua 1:8). Even before that, God said, "And these words, which I command thee this day, shall be in thy heart" (Deuteronomy 6:6). Our Lord set an example to us when He was able to quote the Scriptures to ward off the onslaught of Satan (Matthew 4:1-11). The psalmist knew the secret of victory over sin when he said, "Thy word have I hid in mine heart, that I might not sin against thee" (Psalm 119:11). Not only does hiding the Word in our hearts help us individually but it also enables us to speak authoritatively to those who would challenge us or ask why we believe as we do. ". . . and be ready always to give an answer to every man that asketh you a reason of the hope that is in you" (I Peter 3:15). "So shall I have wherewith to answer him that reproacheth me: for I trust in thy word" (Psalm 119: 42). The Word of God is the staff of life to us and we must feed upon it through meditation and memory and be able to present the heavenly manna to others.

The faculty of memory is one of the greatest gifts God has ever given to man. Without it there could be no knowledge, for, in the last analysis, the accumulation of knowledge depends upon memory. In spite of that fact, the average person belittles his memory. He laughingly says, "I have a memory like a sieve" and dismisses any possibility of his memorizing anything. Strictly speaking, there is no such generality as a good memory or a bad one. Some are more retentive than others in certain areas because of special interests or concentrated efforts. Most of the sluggish memories are so because they have been neglected. They need to be challenged by an interesting subject.

Carl Seashore, an eminent psychologist, has said, "The average man does not use above ten percent of his actual inherited capacity for memory. He wastes the ninety percent by violating the natural laws of remembering." The memory does not deteriorate with age but only through disuse. The arm, or any part of the physical body, would wither and become weak if it were not used. It is kept strong by usage. The same is true of the memory. Thomas DeQuincy the famous English essayist said, "The memory strengthens as you lay burdens upon it and becomes trustworthy as you trust it."

The person who envies another with a vast storehouse of scriptural knowledge must be made aware of one fact. The memory is like a savings bank. You cannot draw upon it unless you have made deposits. The Spirit of God works with our memory and "bring[s] all things to [our] remembrance" (John 14:26). He brings back to us the things we have put at His disposal in the storehouse of our minds. Thus it is essential that we use the memory God has given us in the way He intended.

If a person says he cannot memorize, it is that very attitude that is his greatest barrier. He sabotages his memory by saying it cannot be done. The greatest factor in breaking that mental block is honestly to want to commit something to memory. It is a proven fact that the memory recalls most easily that information in which the person is most vitally interested. The musician can remember musical scores, the engineer recalls complicated figures, and the sports fan can remember batting averages. Half the battle is having an intense interest in the subject. The person who cannot remember names is basically not interested in people. If he persistently forgets (or never gets) a name, he actually counts the man and his name as being unimportant. No wonder it is an insult to forget a person's name!

The Christian who wants to know the Scriptures and be able to quote them can do so. That strong desire is the starting point. Then, with a basic knowledge of the process of memory and some diligent effort, he is on his way to being a walking Bible.

When you start to memorize Scripture portions, set a goal for yourself. Make it realistic and strive to keep on the schedule you have set. Such a method produces results in any realm of endeavor. It is better to take a small portion and learn it successfully than to be too ambitious and fall short. Count it better to set a goal to memorize two verses a week and do it thoroughly than to strive for one verse a day and fail to reach the goal. Start slowly and when your memorization program gets into gear, and you are adjusted to the pace, you can accelerate it.

You can draw up your own plan, but make it a rule to be consistent. Make it as rigid as if it were imposed upon you by a superior. If you set a given time for this work, do your utmost to meet that schedule regularly. If you are one who lacks time for such a worthy endeavor, then look for the gaps that all of us have in even the busiest day. The time when commuting to and from work, that extra ten minutes during the lunch hour, or those impatient moments while waiting for dinner. Some good licks at memorizing can be gotten in even while doing other tasks that require manual, but no mental, skill. Try it while washing dishes, doing touch-up painting, washing the car, or mowing the lawn. Even the moments while waiting for appointments or for others to appear can be used to good advantage. The main point is to be systematic, rather than slipshod, about this business of memorizing Bible verses.

There are several systems of keeping Bible verses before you in the process of memorizing. Some use the card system and have the text written on one side of a card and the reference on the other. Such cards can be carried on the person and thus made available for memory work or review during unexpected leisure moments. Housewives often place cards in strategic places around the house to be a reminder to memorize when their eyes get a glimpse of the card. Men driving to work put a card above the sun visor and utilize that driving time to hide the Word in heart and mind. Still others will use a small notebook and thus have all the verses together.

A very excellent time for doing memory work or review is just before going to sleep at night. That is an ideal time to center thoughts upon eternal truths; but there are additional advantages also — those who study the workings of the mind assert that the subconscious workings of our thinking faculties can be put to work for us. When concerted efforts are made to memorize just before sleep comes, then the subconscious mind takes over. Like a fireless cooker, it keeps those last thoughts simmering while the person himself is resting. Very often the memorized portion will be the first thought upon waking and it will be fixed in the mind. In addition to a memory help, your last thought of the day (and also the first one) is upon a truth of the Word of God.

The more interesting the subject matter, the easier it is to memorize it. Also the more interesting the method of memorizing, the easier it will be. If this can be done by means of a game or through competition, it will be the more fascinating. When several in a family are all memorizing, each can report to the other or try to outdo the other and the whole process can be fun for all.

Concentration, association, and repetition all play an important part in memory work. An additional factor often overlooked is a space gap between efforts at memorizing and review. That interval allows the thought processes to set somewhat as concrete does as it is drying. More progress is made in learning during three two-minute periods than in one six-minute period. Experimenting will prove that fact. Often you will spend much time concentrating on and repeating a given portion — only to forget it shortly afterward. When you apply yourself diligently to it and then forget it for a time, and return later to concentrate some more, the results will be better. Repetition is important, but break it up with an interval between efforts.

Review is essential for permanently retaining facts in the memory. After you have thoroughly memorized material, make it a point to review it every once in a while to make it the more permanent.

The Bible is full of beautiful gems of truth. You will never want for material to memorize and quote. Choosing the right verses can be most important. It all depends upon your purpose in the memory work. If you want comforting promises to be a consolation in your times of trial and trouble, you will find many of them. If your paramount desire is to have verses to substantiate certain doctrines, you can find them. There is so much from which to choose that you must make a decision right from the beginning as to what you want to memorize first.

The soul winner will single out for memorization the verses that he will be most likely to use in dealing with another on the matter of salvation. He will start with the simple and basic texts and develop his repertoire as he goes along. Eventually he will have a storehouse of scriptural knowledge on the tip of his tongue. That knowledge, coupled with his experience in dealing with individuals about spiritual matters, will be invaluable to him and help to point many to the Saviour.

We are in a spiritual conflict. The most effective weapon at our disposal is "the sword of the Spirit, which is the word of God." To acquit ourselves valiantly as soldiers of the cross, we must become adept in using this sword. Whether we whisk out our Testament at the least provocation or let the words roll from the reservoir of our memory, we must use the truth wisely and adroitly. We must guide the burnished blade of the Bible to the vital spot where our opponent must cry touché.

In our hands we have an instrument that can do a needed job. The Spirit of God can give us wisdom to use it aright. It is our responsibility to ply the sword.

ASSIGNMENTS

Find a spot in your day for regular memorization of Scripture verses. Be prepared to share that information with other class members and perhaps your selected time will give an idea to others.

Purchase and get in the habit of carrying a small New Testament.

5. Steam to Start

SAM JONES used to tell of an experience he had as he was leaving Atlanta for Chattanooga. Before boarding the train he sauntered along the platform toward the engine. He overheard the engineer say to the fireman, "Have you enough steam to start?" After an affirmative reply the engineer said, "Well, we'd better get going then." Jones rushed back to board the coach but what he had overheard lingered long in his mind.

The question was not, "Have you enough steam to get to Chattanooga?" (The boilers could not contain that much.) It was, "Have you enough to start?" Before the trip was one-third over, there was so much steam in the engine that the excess had to be let off. Yet at the beginning only enough to start was needed.

One application of that truth is that no person need have enough grace and strength stored up to enable him to live for God for the remainder of his life. All he needs is enough to start, and he will receive his sustaining portion each day.

In spite of the fact that knowledge can be stored up, the personal worker need not delay his soul winning activities until he has a thorough knowledge of the Bible and methods of personal evangelism. If he were to wait that long, he would never get started. Probably more sincere people delay their witnessing because of a feeling of inadequacy than for any other reason. But you will never come to the place where you feel you have adequate knowledge or experience. The basic essential and probably the hardest part is to start. You can learn more through a few minutes of practical experience than through ten times that period spent in cramming and preparing. The key is to have a combination of the two.

The ministerial student does not spend years studying, then receive a diploma, and suddenly become a preacher. Even in school he tries his wings and mixes the books with the practical experiences. If he is a capable minister of the gospel upon graduation, it is because he started preaching before he felt he was adequately trained or had a sufficient storehouse of knowledge. The only way to learn to preach is by preaching. The same is true of personal soul winning. If an individual refused to preach until he was perfectly trained, he would never do so. The individual who thinks he must know all the answers before he speaks to a soul about Christ might as well give up the idea completely.

When you finish this book you will still have a feeling of inadequacy. If you absorb these truths thoroughly there will still be much you will not know about this subject. It will be necessary to take faltering steps and then lean upon the Holy Spirit. Begin now. At this stage of your experience it is not a question of having enough steam stored up for the entire journey. Do you have enough to start? Starting is the most important part of this great work of evangelism. By the grace of God you can start now.

If you had to be familiar with only five Bible verses to be a soul winner, could you be one? If knowing those references, being able to turn to them, understanding their basic teachings, or memorizing them were all that were required to get a diploma, could you qualify? That sounds too simple but it actually is all that is needed. The rudimentary facts about salvation can be known and taught through five simple verses from the Bible. Once you know them you are ready to start.

When you know those five verses, your learning days will not be over. You will not have the Bible background of those who have spent a lifetime studying the blessed Book or the composure of the person who has been winning souls for thirty years. You will still be confronted with hard questions and have difficult situations. But you are ready to *start* and that is what you want to do.

Here are those verses and this is the time to become familiar with them:

1. ROMANS 3:23 — *"For all have sinned, and come short of the glory of God."*

A man must realize that he needs a Saviour before you can present the Saviour to him. This plain statement declares that all are sinners and, hence, all need a Saviour. Other portions of the Scriptures verify this truth and can be used as further corroboration. Romans 11:32 says, "For God hath concluded them all in unbelief, that he might have mercy upon all." Paul declares a similar truth, "But the scripture hath concluded all under sin, that the promise by faith of Jesus Christ might be given to them that believe" (Galatians 3:22). Solomon, the wise man, said, "For there is not a just man upon earth, that doeth good, and sinneth not" (Ecclesiastes 7:20).

In Romans 3:22 we read: ". . . for there is no difference." This is not to infer that all men are identical in every way. Neither does it hint that all are guilty of the same number or degree of sins. There are definitely some transgressions that are worse and more heinous than others. Some people are respectable sinners and some are despicable ones. One person can wallow in filth and unrighteousness and another commit only one small offense. But there is no difference because both have sinned and come short of the glory of God. Both are sinners. Both need a Saviour.

When a person starts defending himself by saying he is not really a bad sort of a person, he must be reminded that the degree of sin is irrelevant. It is not how terrible a sinner he is but just that he is a sinner. It is not whether he is better than most people but rather that he has come short of the glory of God. A colorful definition of sin is *missing the mark*. That presents an interesting picture of an archer or rifleman engaged in target practice. He may miss the bull's eye by a quarter of an inch or by eight inches. The degree of miss matters less than that he has missed the mark for which he was aiming. He either hits the mark or misses it. If a person sins, in even the most minor way, he is a sinner as much as the one who commits multiple and grave offenses. If he breaks only one commandment he is as guilty as if he had broken them all. "For whosoever shall keep the whole law, and yet offend in one point, he is guilty of all" (James 2:10).

There are many people who are apparently horrified at the least intimation they are sinners. They cite their own definition of a sinner and then protest that their good life could hardly be described in such terms. Generally they tally their comparative goodness and all they have done or refrained from doing. They do so with a tone of finality as if that settles the issue. One question that will befuddle their reasoning is, "Have you ever committed the slightest sin or done something wrong at any time in your life?" Any honest person must answer that question in the affirmative and by doing so admit that he is a sinner. Then a reminder of James 2:10 will leave him standing in need of a Saviour.

Sin has a way of bringing with it a guilt complex. Many who deny being sinners and assert they will get to heaven as quickly as anyone else are putting on a front that they themselves don't even believe. They are only hoping that what they are saying is or will be true. Every individual knows that he is a sinner and depraved before God, whether or not he will always admit it. Someone has said, "We are not so depraved as not to know we are depraved."

I was told that one of my parishioners had been an atheist before his conversion. One day he referred to that period in his life. He said, "You know, I didn't use to believe there was a God. I had some pretty good arguments, too. I loved to argue. I am sure that I convinced many a person that there was no Supreme Being." After a brief pause he added, "You know, there was one fellow, however, that I couldn't convince. Try as I would I could not banish God from his thoughts." Then in a most interesting way he said, "That fellow was myself."

All the while he was apparently convincing others, he himself was not convinced. In like manner those who boldly deny being sinners cannot escape an inner consciousness that they are unworthy to stand in the presence of a holy God.

The Word of God is clear. Anyone who comes short of the perfection as found in the glory of God is a sinner. The Bible says all are found in that status. Therefore all need a Saviour. In the face of what the Bible says, how can the sinner deny his status?

2. ROMANS 6:23 — "For the wages of sin is death; but the gift of God is eternal life through Jesus Christ our Lord."

In this oft-repeated verse is the very epitome of the whole gospel. Many times the more familiar verses that we can quote by rote memory are the ones to which we give little thought in meditation. Thus, in our haste to speak words, we overlook glorious truths.

Basically this verse brings out the truth of salvation by way of contrast. Three contrasts stand out as mountains do on a relief map. Standing in juxtaposition one to another are sin and God, death and life, and wages and gift. In them we view two masters, sin or God; two destinies, death or life; and two alternatives for man to receive, wages or a gift. Man has the prerogative of choosing between them. The responsibility of that choice must be brought to the attention of the sinner. For a sermon on this text, A. G. Brown uses the long but descriptive title: "Hard Work and Bad Pay, or No Work and a Rich Reward."

The wages we receive we justly deserve. They are what we have earned or have coming to us. It is the law of both the universe and God that the wages of sin is death. Those wages are accumulative and proportionate to our sin. Death could have been called the punishment for sin but wages more aptly describes death as something due the sinner.

A gift is directly opposite to wages. It is something presented out of the good will of the donor and with no merit on the part of the recipient. The only condition attached is a willingness on the part of the recipient to receive it. The more accurate translation of this verse makes it read "the free gift of God." Eternal life is God's free gift. It is His own peculiar gift and His best gift. No man possesses that gift by nature and no man can procure it by himself. The marvel is that the gift is wrapped up in God's Son, Jesus Christ, and can be had in fullness by just accepting Him.

The sinner is offered two alternatives. He can choose the wages or the gift. He can choose mastery over his life by sin or by God. For eternity, he can choose either life or death. G. Campbell Morgan has aptly said, "A man can ultimately escape from either sin or grace, but not from both. He can escape from sin by yielding to grace, or he can put himself outside the operation of grace by yielding to sin."

It is only logical that this verse presenting the solid truth of salvation should be used in pointing men to Christ. The black backdrop of death vividly shows the simple gift of salvation through Jesus Christ our Lord.

3. JOHN 1:12 — *"But as many as received him, to them gave he power to become the sons of God, even to them that believe on his name."*

So many times the Scriptures state majestic truths in such simple language. This is one of those times. The essence of gospel truth is that one becomes a son of God by receiving Jesus Christ.

This verse (and the one previous to it) describes two companies of people. Jesus' own group, the Jews, rejected Him, but there were others who received Him. The Jews were religious, were chosen, and had every natural advantage. The other group was a hodgepodge as far as religion was concerned, but they all became sons of God. The difference between curse and blessing lay in the rejection or acceptance of Jesus Christ. Nothing is simpler than that. All other matters take a secondary place to whether or not a person receives Him.

Christianity is Christ, and salvation is a Saviour.

We are not saved by creeds, dogmas, doctrines, actions, beliefs, or by living a certain type of life. We are saved by a person, Jesus Christ. Whether or not we become children of God hinges upon our acceptance or rejection of Him.

The only begotten Son of God has the power to make us sons of God with Him. He has actually transferred to us that authority. Those who believe on Him are given the authority to become children of God through faith in His name. We do not merely take His name, follow in His footsteps, or abide by His teachings. Through accepting Him we have the power actually to become children of God.

When one who is alienated from God is able to become a child of God — that is salvation. And salvation comes to the one who accepts Christ. What a blessed thought and a glorious experience.

A more sobering thought reminds us that, if there is eternal life in accepting Christ, then there is eternal death in rejecting Him. The verse that so clearly sets forth this truth is an excellent one to use in presenting Christ to needy individuals.

4. REVELATION 3:20 — *"Behold, I stand at the door, and knock: if any man hear my voice, and open the door, I will come in to him, and will sup with him, and he with me."*

Possibly no verse so graphically pictures the infinite condescension of Christ as this particular one. We can imagine man knocking at Heaven's portals and seeking admission; but the Son of God knocking at the door of the human heart poses a surprising picture. He stands there thwarted and frustrated. The Creator of the universe begs His creation to free the latch and grant Him admission. There is no commandeering, no force, no compulsion or even persuasion. He is entirely at the mercy of a man. Whether or not He, the Son of God, comes in is determined by the attitude of one mortal being, and yet He stands there with enduring patience, love, and earnestness. The King of Glory deigns to have fellowship with sinful man and awaits an invitation to enter. Such condescension is beyond expression of language.

A simple picture is presented by this text. Jesus Christ is outside the heart, not within. He wants to enter, but a human will withstands Him. If an attitude of indifference persists, He will do nothing to force His way. Whether He enters and brings the joys and blessings of salvation depends entirely upon the attitude of the man himself.

Hear the throbbing call that comes from the lips of the Son of God, "If *any* man hear my voice." It matters not how unworthy the person may be, how deep the stains of his past sin, whether or not he has prestige, or whether even a shred of good can be found in his life. The only requisite is that he hear the voice of the Son of God and swing wide the door of his heart. Anyone who will do that will be saved.

Jesus knocks at the heart door because if admitted there He has access to the whole man. In His great condescension, He bids for all men and all there is of man.

Christ can be beautifully presented through this gem of the Scriptures.

5. ACTS 2:38 — *"Then Peter said unto them, Repent, and be baptized every one of you in the name of Jesus Christ for the remission of sins, and ye shall receive the gift of the Holy Ghost."*

This verse was the clincher for the memorable sermon that Peter preached on the day of Pentecost. Empowered by the Holy Spirit, he defended the actions of the believers, quoted from the prophets, and related the account of the crucifixion, resurrection, and ascension. To put on the capstone and press for a decision he spoke these forthright words. The results speak for themselves, inasmuch as three thousand people were converted. The truth he spoke then is just as effective today, so we can use it.

The call for repentance has not sounded forth as loudly in our day as in generations of the past. However, it is just as essential now as it was then. In the Greek language two words are translated *repent.* One means *change of mind* and the other *concern of soul* or *sorrow.* Although *change of mind* sounds weak, it embraces a change of attitude toward the Lord Jesus Christ which results in a change of inner life. It brings about a turning from sin to God. It speaks of a heart being broken for sin and by sin. There is no conflict between repentance and faith. They actually go hand in hand.

Peter calls not only for repentance but for baptism

as well. Baptism is an outward symbol of true repentance. Both of those steps are incumbent upon individuals and obligatory upon all. He said, "Every one of you."

This verse gives a scriptural command to repent, calls for an outward evidence of that inward work, and then holds forth the promise of the infilling of the Holy Spirit. What more can we present to those with whom we come in contact?

David, the shepherd boy, went against the giant Goliath, with five smooth stones as ammunition. Whatever his motive in having five, when one did the job, we do not know. That is a minor matter. He went forth with that which seemed small and inconsequential but with God's help he did what others could not do. You have five polished stones in these basic verses for soul winning. There can be victory over the seemingly insurmountable giants around you if you trust in God and use your trusty single-shot sling. Let others man the machine guns; you can slay giants with five smooth stones. As you step forth to battle, say with David, "I am come to thee in the name of the Lord of hosts." Then expect the victories that will surely come.

ASSIGNMENTS

Memorize the five basic Scripture verses in this chapter.

Make at least two attempts at personal work, just as if you were a veteran at it. Be prepared to report on your attempts at the next class meeting.

6. Contact!

IN THE EVER-CHANGING ENGLISH LANGUAGE common words very often take on new meanings. The burgeoning aviation industry has added its portion of new definitions to a live and colorful language. When all preparatory details for a flight have been made, the pilot calls to his mechanic but one word, "Contact!" It is as if he is giving information and also a command. By that simple word he is declaring that the ignition switch has been closed, contact is made for the electrical current, and it is time for the propellors to turn. That contact is actually the beginning of a flight or mission and a most important part of it.

Probably the most important aspect of soul winning is the initial step, the approach that is made to the individual. How and when that contact is made, what is said and how it is said, greatly affects the decision that is eventually made, whether to accept Christ or to reject Him. Salesmen say that the approach or contact goes a long way toward making or breaking a sale. The use of proper words, spacing the remarks, inflections of voice, even the tone and attitude have a vital bearing upon what happens. Because of that, too much care cannot be taken in anticipating the approach and making every effort to execute it in the most effective way.

The best blanket advice for making an initial contact with a needy soul is that the approach be filled with tact and wisdom. Tact is that peculiar ability to deal with others without giving offense. It embodies discernment of that which is appropriate and proper under all circumstances. If a personal worker makes a tactful approach to an individual, he stands a good chance of having an attentive listener. If he doesn't, his knowledge or good intentions are to no avail, as he will have no one to listen to the truth he may have to offer.

In the study of the continued evolution of words and their meanings, there is a hint of a very intriguing truth. The words *tact* and *contact* stem from the same original word. Both basically pertained to the verb *touch,* but *tact* then shifted to mean *to touch with feeling* and then eventually to its current definition. In the similarity of the words is a blessed thought. The prefix *con* is often used to indicate *with.* In tracing the history of the word *contact,* one is led to believe that it could mean *with tact.* That gives a strong emphasis to the truth that the approach or contact of the personal worker to the prospective Christian should be made "with tact." Let us give careful consideration as to just how we can tactfully approach those to whom we witness.

Basically there are three major situations in which the soul winner will find himself. In some ways they are similar and in others they are not. They get progressively easier and the third one requires less tact and ingenuity than do the first and second. A person should be prepared to face any one of these situations and be able to start from the circumstances at hand.

1. WHERE CONTACT IS MADE WITH A PERSON TOTALLY UNKNOWN

An outstanding example of this is the account of Jesus approaching the Samaritan woman by the well. He had never met her and she had no idea who He was. His method of contact with her was indeed exemplary as we shall observe in a later chapter. Such modern day contacts are made in speaking to another passenger on a train or plane, in the waiting room at the dentist's office, or to the fisherman sitting nearby on the pier.

In this situation the witness must start a conversation, establish a rapport, and eventually direct the conversation to the things of Jesus Christ. Each step calls for alertness, tact, and wisdom. These God-given abilities can be cultivated and developed.

2. WHERE SOCIAL CONTACT ALREADY EXISTS BUT WHERE THE SUBJECT OF CHRIST MUST BE BROACHED

This situation would exist at a family gathering, a class reunion, or when visiting the home of an old friend. Conversation is already flowing freely and a long-standing rapport exists. There is no need first to gain the confidence of the prospect because that confidence has been previously established. The greatest problem is to stem the tide of rambling words and idle thoughts long enough to speak of vital matters in the light of eternity.

3. WHERE THE PROSPECT IS ANTICIPATING A WORD ABOUT CHRIST

This is the easiest situation of all. It may occur less frequently than the others but it will afford better opportunities. Perhaps, having heard of the conversion of the witness or of his activity in a given church, the prospect asks questions. Nicodemus seeking out Jesus is an example of this situation. Anyone can do personal work under those circumstances, particularly if there is the slightest degree of sincerity behind the questions.

Some individuals are far more aggressive than others in soul winning. Some make opportunities for witnessing and others wait for them. Some say it is God's business to provide the opening, while others feel that God has given them ability to do that. Because of the natural tendency to become passive in this work, it is better to be called an "eager beaver" in this matter than to slip into the rut of complacency.

In any situation there are two major methods of starting a particular course of conversation. The usual course is to bring up the subject at an appropriate time. The other is better if worked properly. It calls for a sentence calculated to bring a response or, preferably, to cause the person to ask a question — thus he starts the subject himself. In some instances it may involve an object that will call forth that question.

To forestall the conversation becoming a monologue when it develops a religious tenor, it is good to ask a question. Experienced witnesses vouch for such a procedure. When Philip approached the Ethiopian eunuch he asked a question, "Understandest thou what thou readest?" (Acts 8:30). When Jesus approached the man at the pool of Bethesda, His first word was a question, "Wilt thou be made whole?" (John 5:6). He did the same to the blind man when He asked, "What wilt thou that I should do unto thee?" (Mark 10:51). Asking a question elicits an answer and is a very good starting point.

Any such question should be a calculated rather than a casual one. Instead of asking a person if he is a Christian, it is better to ask a question which infers that he is not. If he has a personal knowledge of the Saviour he will pick that hint up immediately and give a clear testimony. If he is not a Christian he will probably admit it, and the opening wedge has been effective. Such an admission is the first step in leading a soul to the Lord. Dr. C. S. Lovett often uses a question that is a classic example of this very thing: "Have you ever thought of becoming a Christian?" Note that the inference is that the person is not a Christian. In this nominally Christian country, the average person assumes an individual is a Christian unless he declares he is not. According to the Bible standard we should assume all are not Christians unless a clear-cut statement to the contrary is forthcoming.

Another successful method is to thrust a statement into a casual conversation that will almost always cause the other person to ask a particular question. That question will then open the subject. Carlton Booth suggests a good example of such a statement. If the subject of marriage comes up, or the conversation is steered in that direction, say, "That is the second greatest decision you will ever make in your life." If referring to a marriage in the past, use the past tense of the verb. Invariably the person will say, "What is the most important one?" Then comes the opportunity to declare it is the decision to accept or reject Jesus Christ. Even in using a question to make a contact, you might ask: "What is the greatest decision you have had to make in your lifetime?" Some of the initial replies may seem minor and they might even strike the prospect in that way after he has been told the greatest of all decisions.

Very often successful personal workers have hit upon a gimmick to get individuals to ask a question and thus lay themselves open for a brief word about the Saviour. It is not uncommon to see a man with a gold fishhook on the lapel of his coat. Invariably a person's curiosity is aroused about the meaning of the emblem and the assumption is made that it signifies membership in some fishermen's group. Usually a person will say, "You must be quite a fisherman." Then the witness has his opening and replies, "Well, I'm really not so much of a fisherman as I am a fisher of men." By that time the opening wedge for a spiritual message has entered the conversation. The Men's Fellowship of the Assemblies of God has made such a fishhook a part of their lapel emblem for the very purpose of giving the men an opportunity to witness for Christ. Under that system the prospect usually opens the conversation himself.

Mr. Otis G. Jones, of Fort Wayne, Indiana, is successful both as a salesman and a winner of souls. He has hit upon a plan that gives him a great opportunity to bring men to a decision for Christ. One of the products he sells is a very excellent mechanical pencil. He does not sell to individuals but in large quantities to huge industrial firms. For his own use in soul winning, each year he buys a thousand dollars' worth of those pencils, with a Scripture verse printed on the barrel.

If you saw Otis Jones, probably the first thing that would catch your eye would be four or five identical pencils in the breast pocket of his coat. If you react like the average individual, you'd ask, "Why do you need so many pencils?" He wouldn't be surprised because he is always answering that question. He'd tell you, "I carry them just so people will ask that." Then he would continue, "This pencil is the very best one on the market and I'm going to give you one of them." With that opening wedge he launches into a brief sales pitch, as if he were talking to one of his best prospects for a quantity sale. He demonstrates that no matter how hard you push on it you cannot break the lead. He steps on the cap to show it will hold the weight of a man without breaking. He tells about its having a year's supply of eraser. "But the outstanding feature of this pencil is that it tells you how to get to heaven," says Jones; and when the prospect looks puzzled, he reads the Scripture verses on the barrel — Ephesians 2:8-9. By that time the subject of pencils is forgotten and Jones speaks of the things of God and presses for a decision. Since his conversion in 1950, he has won many, including a prominent United States Senator, to Christ through this system.

If a common item like a pencil can provide an opening wedge for witnessing, then there are many other mundane objects that can be used to get men to ask questions and step into a situation to receive the gospel truth.

A splendid way to direct a conversation to spiritual matters is by letting common objects speak of spiritual truths. That can be done in the early stages of a conversation or at any time. It is accepted that there are sermons in stones. By the parables that He presented, Jesus demonstrated that the ordinary things of life can be used to illustrate profound spiritual truths. He taught the truths of the Kingdom by referring to a farmer scattering seed, a runaway boy, a lily, a sparrow, a little child, or a fig tree. When He desired to speak to a Samaritan woman about spiritual matters, He talked about water and then later referred to living water of which one can drink and never thirst again. The art of linking natural objects to the spiritual, and bringing forth truth, is most effective. Be on the alert for anything that can be used in that way. It is surprising how many objects can serve in such a manner.

The late Dr. Charles S. Price told of how a small object was an instrument in winning both a man and his wife to the Lord. Dr. Price had gone to a store to get a ruler. While he was standing at the stationery counter, ruler in hand, waiting for the salesgirl, a friendly man standing nearby said, "That looks like a good ruler."

"I know a better one," answered Price.

"Which one?"

"The Golden Rule."

"The Golden Rule? What's that?" asked the puzzled stranger.

With that Dr. Price quoted the words of Jesus which are often called the Golden Rule (Luke 6: 31). As a result of that conversation the man accepted an invitation to the Price evangelistic meetings and he and his wife were gloriously converted. Who would think that an ordinary ruler could be an instrument in winning two souls?

It is a part of discretion to approach an individual through something in which he is interested. Too often we converse about the things that interest us but are of no concern to others. The avid fisherman can be touched through the vernacular of his passion for leisure hours. The sports enthusiast will be interested in the spiritual experience of Bob Richards, the champion pole vaulter, while it would have lesser weight with someone who doesn't know the difference between the shot put and the discus. He who cultures roses can be interested by the question, "You are a horticultural expert. Do you know what person has been called the Rose of Sharon?" To the insurance salesman talk about long term coverage — for eternity. To the businessman talk about profit and loss — "What shall it profit a man?" Every man has interests that are the soft spot of his armor. Good common sense dictates that such a spot be used in the initial contact with him. If the witness has a common interest with the prospect, it is just that much better. He can use their common ground to win that man for God.

A proven approach to any individual is that of honest commendation. If you know anything about a person upon which you can pay a compliment, then do it. It should not be a trumped up compliment that is vapid and weak. Don't use commendation at all if it is going to be evident that it is not honest. Do so only if you are sincere. That doesn't mean that his achievement must be in an area that you endorse. His hogs may have won the blue ribbon at the county fair, or he may have been chosen the top real estate salesman of the week, or he may even have been the winner of a prize for guessing the number of beans in a jar at a nearby market. Compliment and commend a person when you can and then let it be a stepping-stone to more important words.

A clear example of such a policy is found in the Scriptures (Acts 17:22-28). The apostle Paul was in Athens and wanted to preach Christ to those Stoics and Epicureans. He stood at the Parthenon on Mars Hill, amidst all the idols of which the Greeks were so proud. There were images of Jupiter, Apollo, Bachus, Saturn, Mars, Mercury, Venus, Vesta, Minerva, Diana, and a host of others. How would he preach Christ amid such a heathen display? If he were in a Jewish synagogue he would read an Old Testament portion and preach from it. He had often done that. That would not work here, however.

Both the Jews and the Christians accepted the writings of the prophets, but the Greeks did not.

He started his sermon in a strange way. He complimented the people on the great collection of idols. They beamed when he did that because the display was their pride and joy. He called attention to one empty niche with the inscription, "To the Unknown God." They explained that they did not want to overlook any one deity and, hence, that niche and inscription. "That's the very God I have come to preach about," said Paul. With that he presented to them the full truth of Jesus Christ.

Some people would count it a compromise to preach amid idols, to say nothing of paying a compliment upon an extensive collection of them. Paul took his text from a heathen inscription and used it to preach Christ to an idolatrous people. His compliment opened the door for his masterful sermon.

There is a difference of opinion as to the value of a carried Bible as an opening wedge for a conversation. If riding on a train, would you open and read your Bible with the secondary purpose of inciting a question from one near by? Will the sight of an open or carried Bible attract or repel?

Generally speaking, the sight of such a Bible will attract some people and repel others. It will attract the Christian or even the nominal church member. It will also attract the person who is in desperate straits and needs help badly. For other people it will throw up a barrier and forestall any possibility of a conversation.

In England the majority of the Protestant ministers wear clerical collars such as those worn by priests in this country. Among many ministers there is a debate as to whether such a collar has its advantages or disadvantages. Somewhat like the carried or open Bible, it will attract some people and repel others. The question is, which advantage will outweigh the other?

A personal worker should always have a small Testament on his person. He must use it in his soul winning. Whether or not it should be in sight before the contact or in an attempt to make the contact is something to be decided for each occasion.

Many personal soul winners use suitable tracts in connection with their efforts. Such tracts are an effective means of getting out the gospel. Many testimonies can be given of conversions brought about through the printed page. The matter of using tracts as an opening wedge for soul winning is just a little different situation. If a person hands out a tract and then lets the printed page do its own work, that is one thing; but if he follows it up with personal conversation, it is another.

In the latter situation the tract should be a very brief one. It ought to have a catchy title and should preferably arouse the curiosity of the reader. It should be brief enough to be read hurriedly at the moment and leave time for the usual contact of the witness. Several such tracts combining brief copy and pictures have been published and have been used most effectively.

When contact is made with an unsaved person, the witness can be most effective when he has a clear objective in mind. What is his purpose or goal? Is he out just to witness to someone or is he attempting to bring that person to a decision? Some take the attitude that they must merely clear their own soul of a responsibility by handing out a tract or saying a brief word to a passing individual. Their aim is merely to drop a little seed rather than pause in an attempt to do a bit of reaping.

For the most part, the soul winner must do more than merely tell people the truth. He must do it in such a way as to bring the person into the fold of God. His goal should be beyond that of bearing witness of the Word. The ultimate aim is to win the prospect to Christ. Like a salesman, he must make efforts to close the sale and end the transaction in complete victory. That is not always possible, but every effort should be made toward that end.

Solomon, who knew something of wisdom, said, ". . . he that winneth souls is wise" (Proverbs 11: 30). The objective is not merely to witness but to win souls. Witnessing is but a means to the end of garnering in the souls of men. Winning souls is a skillful process halfway between using force and coercion and just speaking the truth and caring nothing for the results.

Like the hunter stalking his prey, or the fisherman outwitting the denizens of the deep, the soul winner plays a skillful game but with much higher stakes — the eternal souls of men. His play calls for skill and strategy. He is not only baiting a hook or a trap. He is not merely recording the contacts he has made and the pieces of literature he has handed out. The contacts are important, but they are not the end. They are the opening that will bring about the desired results.

You may not win to Christ every soul that you set out to snare. The reasons may be many and varied. Let not one of those reasons be that you made a faulty approach to a needy soul.

ASSIGNMENT

Make at least three attempts to bring Christ into conversations that are centered on other subjects. Use the ideas suggested in this chapter, such as asking a question, making a statement that will provoke a question, or letting some natural object suggest the spiritual. Record and be prepared to report on your experiences.

7. Nine Pillars

THE ACCOMPLISHED SOUL WINNER, like the man who is a success in any endeavor, must continually expand his knowledge and improve his technique. He may win souls with but a meager knowledge of the Bible, but that should not hinder his further pursuit or command of scriptural understanding. In a previous chapter it has been stated that souls can be pointed to the Saviour through the quotation of five simple Bible verses. That is a beginning point but by no means the end. Use those verses in practical witnessing, but at the same time be memorizing and becoming familiar with other Scripture verses.

Nine facts form the substructure of all personal evangelism. To the Christian they are elementary; but it is essential that he know them and be able to pass them on to any prospect, if that person is to be led to Christ. Sturdier than granite and as unshakable as Gibralter, these pillars of truth are backed by Scripture references from all parts of the Bible. The diligent witness will become so conversant with these nine facts and their corroborating verses that he can use any or all of them at the least provocation.

1. ALL MEN ARE SINNERS AND HENCE LOST

The little word *all* must be strongly emphasized. Paul says, "For *all* have sinned, and come short of the glory of God" (Romans 3:23). In another place he argues, ". . . and so death passed upon *all* men, for that *all* have sinned" (Romans 5:12). To the Galatians he wrote, "But the scripture hath concluded *all* under sin, that the promise by faith of Jesus Christ might be given to them that believe" (Galatians 3:22).

If a person lays claim to righteousness and protests his being called a sinner, a sure mouth-stopper is another verse from the pen of the great apostle. "As it is written, There is none righteous, no, not one: There is none that understandeth, there is none that seeketh after God. They are all gone out of the way, they are together become unprofitable; there is none that doeth good, no, not one" (Romans 3: 10-12). Although some boldly claim that they have never sinned, the Scriptures contradict such a statement. "If we say that we have no sin, we deceive ourselves, and the truth is not in us" (I John 1:8). That takes care of the present, and a following verse refers to the past. "If we say that we have not sinned, we make him a liar, and his word is not in us" (I John 1:10). To acknowledge the presence of sin is to be confronted with the consequences of sin. Jesus said, "Whosoever committeth sin is the servant of sin" (John 8:34). As such a slave one can only look forward to inevitable consequences. "For the wages of sin is death" (Romans 6:23).

It is folly to assume that one must do something

extremely wicked to be lost. The sinner is already lost and he must do something to escape that condition. ". . . he that believeth not is condemned already, because he hath not believed in the name of the only begotten Son of God" (John 3:18). To emphasize this truth further, Jesus said, ". . . if ye believe not that I am he, ye shall die in your sins" (John 8:24).

All men are sinners and as such are in a lost state. The only escape is through faith in Christ. To reject Him is to remain lost, but to accept Him is to be saved. "He that hath the Son hath life; and he that hath not the Son of God hath not life" (I John 5:12).

2. CHRIST DIED TO SAVE SINNERS

The essence of the gospel is found in I Corinthians 15:3-4: "For I delivered unto you first of all that which I also received, how that Christ died for our sins according to the scriptures; and that he was buried, and that he rose again the third day." Because all men are sinners and in an ungodly state, it was necessary that He die to redeem us. "For when we were yet without strength, in due time Christ died for the ungodly" (Romans 5:6). The apostle Paul again expresses this truth by writing, "For God hath not appointed us to wrath, but to obtain salvation by our Lord Jesus Christ, who died for us" (I Thessalonians 5:9-10). Jesus Himself foretold His plan when He said, "I am the good shepherd: the good shepherd giveth his life for the sheep" (John 10:11). John not only tells of

Christ's death but also of what our responsibility should be because of it. "Hereby perceive we the love of God, because he laid down his life for us: and we ought to lay down our lives for the brethren" (I John 3:16).

The blood of Jesus Christ speaks of His death and hence is essential to the salvation of man. Here are two plain references: ". . . ye were not redeemed with corruptible things, as silver and gold . . . but with the precious blood of Christ" (I Peter 1:18-19); "In whom we have redemption through his blood, the forgiveness of sins" (Ephesians 1:7; Colossians 1:14).

The shedding of His blood and His death were for the purpose of redeeming sinners, and that means us all. ". . . Christ Jesus came into the world to save sinners" (I Timothy 1:15). ". . . thou shalt call his name Jesus: for he shall save his people from their sins" (Matthew 1:21). "For the Son of man is come to save that which was lost" (Matthew 18:11).

This truth can best be summed up by John's statement, ". . . God sent his only begotten Son into the world, that we might live through him. Herein is love, not that we loved God, but that he loved us, and sent his Son to be the propitiation for our sins" (I John 4:9-10).

3. Christ is the exclusive way of salvation

Everyone will agree that Jesus Christ was a good man. Most people admit that He was one of the best individuals that ever lived. He is readily recognized as a noble teacher and example. Many will accept Him as a way-shower. However, when He is presented as the exclusive door to eternal life, people rebel and search frantically for another entrance.

The truth is that Jesus is the exclusive way to heaven and out of sin. Nothing in the Scriptures is clearer than that. He asserted such a truth repeatedly and others who were moved upon to write the Scriptures attest to that vital fact.

Jesus said, "Verily, verily, I say unto you, He that entereth not by the door into the sheepfold, but climbeth up some other way, the same is a thief and a robber" (John 10:1). Then, as if to clinch the truth, He added, "I am the door: by me if any man enter in, he shall be saved, and shall go in and out, and find pasture" (verse 9). He also declared, ". . . I am *the* way, *the* truth, and *the* life: no man cometh unto the Father, but by me" (John 14:6). Notice closely the exclusiveness of the article *the*. He is not *a* way but *the* way.

The apostle Peter boldly preached Jesus Christ to the seemingly religious leaders of Israel and very pointedly reminded them of the exclusive way to God through Him. "Neither is there salvation in any other: for there is none other name under heaven given among men, whereby we must be saved" (Acts 4:12).

In referring to basic facts the apostle Paul reminded the Corinthians, "For other foundation can no man lay than that is laid, which is Jesus Christ" (I Corinthians 3:11). He reminded Timothy that there was only one mediator between God and men. "For there is one God, and one mediator between God and men, the man Christ Jesus" (I Timothy 2:5). Human reasoning would say there are many mediators but the Bible teaches there is only one. Under inspiration of the Spirit of God, Paul even went so far as to assert that those who do not accept Christ are accursed: "If any man love not the Lord Jesus Christ, let him be Anathema" (I Corinthians 16:22).

A résumé of the exclusiveness of Christ as the portal to eternal life is presented in I John 5:11-12: "And this is the record, that God hath given to us eternal life, and this life is in his Son. He that hath the Son hath life; and he that hath not the Son of God hath not life." Eternal life can be obtained exclusively through Jesus Christ.

4. CHRIST IS WILLING TO SAVE ALL

On the basis of merit, not a one of us would or could be saved. However, because salvation is of grace, all have access to Christ. If any fail to lay claim to Him and His blessings, they alone are at fault. Not only has Christ purchased a complete salvation but also He is willing to bestow it upon all who seek Him.

The best news you can give a person who questions Christ's willingness to accept a vile sinner is to quote the Saviour's own words. He said, ". . . him that cometh to me I will in no wise cast out" (John 6:37). That in itself should give assurance to anyone. The apostle Paul reminded Timothy of the broad expanse of the will of God in this matter:

"For this is good and acceptable in the sight of God our Saviour; who will have all men to be saved, and to come unto the knowledge of the truth" (I Timothy 2:3-4). Peter emphasized this fact by saying, "The Lord is . . . not willing that any should perish, but that all should come tò repentance" (II Peter 3:9).

An inspiring example is given in Matthew 8. A leper sought Jesus for physical healing. He prefaced his petition with the sentence, "Lord, if thou wilt, thou canst make me clean." The answer of Jesus was simple and forthright. He said, "I will; be thou clean." The same willingness on the part of the Saviour prevails today.

The plan of salvation, as it pertains to the will of God, is given in Galatians 1:4. Speaking of Christ, it says, "Who gave himself for our sins, that he might deliver us from this present evil world, according to the will of God and our Father." It is God's will that we should thus be delivered.

If we can depend upon any one thing, it is that which God has spoken through His Word. One of the promises that cannot fail is found in I John 1:9: "If we confess our sins, he is faithful and just to forgive us our sins, and to cleanse us from all unrighteousness." The contingency in the little word *if* does not rest upon God's side of the bargain but upon ours. He who wills to confess shall know that God wills to forgive.

Every evidence points to the willingness of God to accept those who have a mind to seek His face in sincerity.

5. WE ARE SAVED BY FAITH

Faith is the element by which we touch God and receive from Him. Some have tried to reach God through the avenues of culture, education, will power, good works, position, abstinence, or feelings, but their efforts have been futile and vain. The Scriptures declare we are saved by faith and by faith alone. What could be clearer than, ". . . by grace are ye saved through faith; and that not of yourselves: it is the gift of God" (Ephesians 2:8)? Romans 3:28 says, "Therefore we conclude that a man is justified by faith without the deeds of the law." In a later chapter it is expressed, "Therefore being justified by faith, we have peace with God through our Lord Jesus Christ" (Romans 5:1).

Men of all generations have striven to do the works of God. They follow such pursuits because they want to be pleasing in His sight. Once when Jesus was on the earth a crowd came to Him asking an age-old question: "What shall we do, that we might work the works of God?" The answer of Jesus startled them and continues to astound many: "This is the work of God, that ye believe on him whom he hath sent" (John 6:28-29). The greatest work that anyone can do to please God is to have faith in His Son.

Those who search for some commandment to obey will find one listed in I John 3:23: "And this is his commandment, That we should believe on the name of his son Jesus Christ, and love one another, as he gave us commandment."

The apostle Paul expressed the sentiment of his

heart by writing, "And be found in him, not having mine own righteousness, which is of the law, but that which is through the faith of Christ, the righteousness which is of God by faith" (Philippians 3:9). He also wrote boldly to the Galatian church: ". . . ye are all children of God by faith in Christ Jesus" (Galatians 3:26).

There is no other way to become a child of God than through faith in Christ. Human schemes and connivings that would supposedly find another means of reaching God are like unfinished bridges. They may appear sound at the beginning but they leave the person dangling in midair.

We are saved by faith and can never escape that fact.

6. GOOD WORKS HAVE NO PART IN OUR SALVATION

Probably the most prevalent fallacy about salvation is that we must do good deeds to merit the smile of God's approval. It is instinctive in the heart of man to want to earn salvation by that which he does or refrains from doing. Each of us likes to feel independent of God and everyone else. The delusion of purchasing salvation by good deeds gives a false sense of independence. Accepting a salvation provided by another makes us dependent upon that person, Jesus Christ. It is most humbling to acknowledge that dependence, and that is why many reject such a plan and attempt to attain salvation by any other way than through Christ.

It seems strange to sound a negative note such as this, yet the Bible does so repeatedly. Human reasoning puts so much emphasis upon the works of the flesh and the deeds of the law that the writers of the Scriptures felt impelled to refute such an idea. It is still necessary to do so. The Scriptures say, "For they being ignorant of God's righteousness, and going about to establish their own righteousness, have not submitted themselves unto the righteousness of God" (Romans 10:3).

When the apostle Paul declared so emphatically that we are saved by faith, he went on to add, "Not of works, lest any man should boast" (Ephesians 2:9). In his other epistles he emphasizes the same point: "Not by works of righteousness which we have done, but according to his mercy he saved us, by the washing of regeneration, and renewing of the Holy Ghost" (Titus 3:5).

Even the good deeds of attempting to keep God's law do not justify us before Him. "Therefore by the deeds of the law shall no flesh be justified in his sight: for by the law is the knowledge of sin" (Romans 3: 20). "Knowing that a man is not justified by the works of the law, but by the faith of Jesus Christ, . . . that we might be justified by the faith of Christ, and not by the works of the law: for by the works of the law shall no flesh be justified" (Galatians 2:16). "Who hath saved us, and called us with a holy calling, not according to our works, but according to his own purpose and grace, which was given us in Christ Jesus before the world began" (II Timothy 1:9).

The person who, by his own works and deeds, attempts to keep the laws of God, suddenly realizes the futility of such attempts when confronted with the words of James: "For whosoever shall keep the whole law, and yet offend in one point, he is guilty of all" (James 2:10). Before we can fully trust in Christ for salvation we must be aware of the vainness of our works and endeavors to obtain salvation on our own behalf.

7. CHRIST IS ABLE TO KEEP AS WELL AS TO SAVE

After the drunkard, Jerry MacAuley, experienced a marvelous conversion, he went to his room to pray. A very real temptation for him were the corner saloons with their pungent, permeating odors. (In those days it was quite common for the proprietors to sprinkle whiskey-soaked sawdust on the sidewalk in front of the saloons, that the aroma might attract passers-by.) Jerry remained in his room for three days, fearful to go out because he must pass some of those saloons. He was getting desperate because he needed food. Suddenly the Spirit of God whispered to him, "If God is able to save, He is able to keep." With that knowledge, MacAuley walked out triumphantly and was undaunted by the fears of the old temptations. Victory was his.

The person who hesitates to accept Christ for fear of his own weakness to live a consistent Christian life needs to comprehend God's promises. As surely as He has promised to save us, so surely has He promised to keep us. Peter, who knew what it was to stumble when he trusted in himself, wrote later of Christians "who are kept by the power of God" (I Peter 1:5). It is most significant that he penned those words, because he learned this truth the hard way. Jude committed the Christians "unto him that is able to keep you from falling" (Jude 24). John says, "'Greater is he that is in you, than he that is in the world" (I John 4:4). In writing to Timothy, the apostle Paul declares triumphantly, ". . . I know who I have believed, and am persuaded that he is able to keep that which I have committed unto him against that day" (II Timothy 1:12). To the church at Thessalonica he wrote, ". . . the Lord is faithful, who shall stablish you, and keep you from evil" (II Thessalonians 3:3). What greater promise could a person want than that?

Whatever the temptations or trials that may come, God's grace is sufficient to keep us in and through them. "And God is able to make all grace abound toward you; that ye, always having all sufficiency in all things, may abound to every good work" (II Corinthians 9:8). "There hath no temptation taken you but such as is common to man: but God is faithful, who will not suffer you to be tempted above that ye are able; but will with the temptation also make a way to escape, that ye may be able to bear it" (II Corinthians 10:13).

Even the weakest new convert can lay claim to the secret of victory as expressed by the apostle Paul, "I can do all things through Christ which strengtheneth me" (Philippians 4:13). As such a person starts to live for Christ, he can start each day by quoting, ". . . The Lord is my helper, and I will not fear what man shall do unto me" (Hebrews 13:6). As he realizes that Christ is a keeper as well as a Saviour, he can lean heavily upon Him.

8. The Christian Must Confess His Lord

It is most difficult, if not impossible, to be a secret follower of the Lord. Many have tried it and have stifled their testimony for one reason or another. The whole idea of such secrecy is contrary to the plan of God and hence such attempts are futile. The message of the Scriptures is straightforward and plain, ". . . if thou shalt confess with thy mouth the Lord Jesus, and shalt believe in thine heart that God hath raised him from the dead, thou shalt be saved. For with the heart man believeth unto righteousness; and with the mouth confession is made unto salvation" (Romans 10:9-10).

Jesus was emphatic about the necessity of witnessing for Him. He said, "Whosoever therefore shall be ashamed of me and of my words in this adulterous and sinful generation; of him also shall the Son of man be ashamed, when he cometh in the glory of his Father with the holy angels" (Mark 8:38). "Whosoever therefore shall confess me before men, him will I confess also before my Father which is in heaven. But whosoever shall deny me before men, him will I also deny before my Father which is in heaven" (Matthew 10:32-33; Luke 12:8-9). Throughout these verses is an inference that we cannot be His followers without confessing Him to others. John suggests the same thing by writing, "Whosoever shall confess that Jesus is the Son of God, God dwelleth in him, and he in God" (I John 4:15).

The genuine Christian is called upon not only to express his position but also to give a reason for his hope. ". . . be ready always to give an answer to every man that asketh you a reason of the hope that is in you" (I Peter 3:15). We also are admonished to interject our testimony into our casual conversation. "Let your speech be alway with grace, seasoned with salt, that ye may know how ye ought to answer every man" (Colossians 4:6).

The apostle Paul, whose testimony rang out so clearly, has set an example for us. He said, "Be not thou therefore ashamed of the testimony of our Lord, . . . but be thou partaker of the afflictions of the gospel according to the power of God" (II Timothy 1:8). He also reminds us of the consequences of our being ashamed of Christ. "If we suffer, we shall also reign with him: if we deny him, he also will deny us" (II Timothy 2:12). The positive testimony of Paul should be that of every child of God. "For I am not ashamed of the gospel of Christ: for it is the power of God unto salvation to everyone that believeth; to the Jew first, and also to the Greek" (Romans 1:16).

9. NEGLECT OF SALVATION IS PERILOUS

More souls have been damned by neglecting salvation than by any other reason. No individual ever has been, or ever will be, saved by having good intentions. The natural man is in a lost condition until he believes on the Lord Jesus Christ. Thus he does not have to do anything to be lost, but he must do something to be saved. If he neglects to believe and accept Christ, the end is calamitous.

A few years ago a simple four-page tract was published. On the first page was the question,

"What must I do to be saved?" and an indication that the answer was on page two. There was found the scriptural answer, "Believe on the Lord Jesus Christ and thou shalt be saved." Page three asked the question, "What must I do to be lost?" and indicated that the answer was on the last page. That page was blank. This was not a printer's error but was calculated to bring a message to the reader. You don't have to do anything to be lost. Just neglect salvation and you face that peril.

An unanswerable question of the Scriptures is found in Hebrews 2:3: "How shall we escape, if we neglect so great salvation?" Because there is no alternate escape, this question is unanswerable. To neglect salvation means to be lost.

In several places in the Book of Hebrews we are warned that now is the time of salvation. "While it is said, To day if ye will hear his voice, harden not your hearts, as in the provocation" (Hebrews 3:15; Hebrews 3:7-9; Hebrews 4:7). Paul quotes from Isaiah and says veritably the same thing. ". . . behold, now is the accepted time; behold, now is the day of salvation" (II Corinthians 6:2).

From the pen of James comes a warning against procrastination and counting on the days of the future. "Go to now, ye that say, To day or to morrow we will go into such a city, and continue there a year, and buy and sell, and get gain: whereas ye know not what shall be on the morrow. For what is your life? It is even a vapour, that appeareth for a little time, and then vanisheth away. For that ye ought to say, If the Lord will, we shall live, and do this, or that" (James 4:13-15).

The mercy of God is extended to us in that there is a way of salvation through Jesus Christ and that the Spirit of God has called us to Him. To neglect that summons is to court death and destruction. "See that ye refuse not him that speaketh. For if they escaped not who refused him that spake on earth, much more shall not we escape, if we turn away from him that speaketh from heaven" (Hebrews 12:25).

Now you have the nine pillars to which all personal soul winning is anchored. Become conversant with all of them and with the Scripture portions that authenticate and corroborate them. They are the foundation for your witnessing, and the results will be in the ratio of your applying yourself to know and be able to quote these truths.

You have not finished this chapter when you have read or even studied it. Keep referring back to it until you have absorbed and veritably exude all these important truths. It is not only important that you know them but also that you bring others to such a knowledge. Only then will God's purpose be fulfilled in your life.

ASSIGNMENT

Become thoroughly conversant with the nine pillars of truth listed in this chapter. Memorize one key verse to substantiate each of those truths. Later you will want to memorize the other verses. It is better to have one good verse for each point and then you can use every one and back it with Scripture even while you are learning the other verses.

8. Plug the Gaps

MAKING EXCUSES is one of the oldest and commonest practices of men. It is particularly prevalent among those who are being pressed to make a decision for Jesus Christ. Often those excuses are feeble, trivial, and absurd, but they are made with a straight face and a supposed tone of sincerity. When a person does not want to do something, one excuse is as good as another. The excuse does not have to stand the test of logic, reason, or the Word of God. It need not satisfy God, fellowmen, or even the person himself. As long as it is an excuse it would seem to suffice. From examples of such excuses it would hardly seem necessary to be consistent. Many individuals put off accepting Christ until a more convenient time and then when approached later they assert it is too late, that they have sinned too much, hardened their heart, or committed the unpardonable sin. Thus, for them, it is either too early or too late and never the right time.

Knowing human nature and how men would react to the great invitation to eternal life, Jesus gave us an illustrative parable in Luke 14:16-24. A great feast was prepared and an invitation extended to the guests. Instead of graciously accepting, "they all with one consent began to make excuse." Their excuses differed but there was unanimity in that they *all* made excuse.

The excuses are given in the parable and each of them is groundless, senseless, and flimsy. One man said, "I have bought a piece of ground, and I must needs go and see it." The logical time to look over property is before you buy it. There is no hurry after the purchase has been made. The second man said, "I have bought five yoke of oxen, and I go to prove them." The same principle is true on this business transaction. If he didn't prove them before he bought them, then he was most unwise. It's too late now. Whether he made a good purchase or was swindled has already been decided. His knowing it could wait a few hours. What's more, you don't prove oxen at night, and that is when this supper was being held. The third excuse smacks of the humorous. "I have married a wife, and therefore I cannot come." Was it that she would not let him come? Why not bring her along? It is true that in Deuteronomy 24:5 provision was made for such a man not going to war, but this was neither war nor business. It was a social engagement.

The things these three men wanted to do were legitimate but hardly worthy excuses for turning down the invitation that came to them. The land, the oxen, and the wife were personal possessions. The men exaggerated their importance and because of that refused the great invitation. The first man was concerned with the cares of wealth, the second with the pursuit of wealth, and the third was bound by earthly attractions.

The veneered excuses of this parable poignantly point up similar ones that are given in response to an opportunity to accept the invitation of Jesus Christ.

In certain parts of the country, jackrabbits or other animals tend to multiply so fast that they are a detriment to the whole area. Periodically a drive is conducted to kill off thousands of them. A huge fence is built that serves the same purpose as the fisherman's net in the sea. Riders then beat the prairies and force the animals in droves into the mesh fence. It is necessary to have a secure fence with mesh so small that no animal can squeeze through. Then the efforts of the riders are not in vain.

In the previous chapter, nine pillars were presented that are anchor posts in all personal soul winning. They are woven and enmeshed together with Scripture portions that substantiate the truths stated and tend to encircle the prospect. So there will be no loophole for escape, it is wise to plug all the little gaps and have a ready answer for any point of reasoning or any excuse that may be given. A good preparation is to anticipate the excuses that individuals will give for not accepting Christ and with Scripture and logic demonstrate the folly of such excuses.

Although the making of excuses is universal and not confined to logic nor reason, still such excuses fall in a certain pattern. Here are the basic ones that the personal soul winner will hear and should be prepared to refute. Some of the Scripture references will be repetitions of those given previously but they are given again as a ready reference under the classification of excuses.

1. I AM SINCERE IN WHAT I BELIEVE

It is amazing how many people believe the doorway to heaven is sincerity alone. They cling to such an idea in spite of the fact that on the pages of the Bible there is no reference to such a theory. Straight thinking would contradict that belief. In even our lowliest traffic laws, ignorance of the law or the evidence of good intentions is ruled out. If you drive south although you fully believe you are going north, you will certainly not reach your destination, in spite of your sincerity. If you would drink the poisonous contents of a bottle, honestly thinking you are taking medicine, would your sincerity make up for your mistake? If you eat toadstools thinking they are mushrooms, the end will be disastrous in spite of your sincerity.

In the Book of Proverbs are two identical verses just a short distance apart. The repetition lends emphasis to the truth. "There is a way which seemeth right unto a man, but the end thereof are the ways of death" (Proverbs 14:12; 16:25). This statement clearly conveys the message that a sincere believer in a wrong belief is headed for disaster, notwithstanding his sincerity. You can be sincere but wrong. You can be sincere and end up in the grip of eternal death. More than human appraisal and acceptance is needed to make the way right and bring a person to the desired destination.

108

Every man is not a law unto himself. His own evaluation of a way as being right does not make it so. The Bible is the standard by which all opinions are tried and upon which they must be based. Charles Simeon has aptly expressed it thus: "Act in reference to your soul as the mariner does in navigating a dangerous sea: He consults his chart and his compass continually; and not contented with thinking himself right, he puts his thoughts to the test, and seeks for evidence that he is right. Then may you hope to avoid the rocks and quicksands on which so many thousands perish; and reach in safety the haven you deisre."

2. THERE ARE TOO MANY HYPOCRITES IN THE CHURCH

This is the most illogical of all excuses and yet it is exceedingly common. It stems from a desire to blame someone else instead of shouldering the responsibility for a lost condition.

In dealing with a person who uses this excuse it is wise to admit that there are hypocritical individuals in the best of churches. However, by what stretch of the imagination that is a legitimate excuse for rejecting Christ is hard to understand. Because there are supposed Christians who are counterfeits does not discredit Christianity. You have never seen a counterfeit three-dollar bill because there is no genuine three-dollar bill. Counterfeits are only imitations of that which is genuine.

There is a sense in which every person stands by himself before God. It is not what others do; but one lives or dies by his own relationship to Christ. How the mistakes or shortcomings of others can alter that relationship is hard to understand.

The Bible is clear on each man's responsibility to God. In Romans 14:11-12 we read, "For it is written, As I live, saith the Lord, every knee shall bow to me and every tongue shall confess to God. So then every one of us shall give account of himself to God."

Salvation is not obtained through the example of others but through Jesus Christ. Whether others fail or walk circumspectly does not affect us. We must answer to God ourselves. The one who is stumbling over the failures of others should be reminded that it is better to be in a church with a few hypocrites (and incidentally setting an example for them) than to spend eternity with a host of such two-faced individuals.

3. IT IS TOO HARD TO BE A CHRISTIAN

The person who uses this excuse is actually confused and befuddled. He does not have an understanding of what it means to be a Christian. He has imagined certain things about a life of which he knows nothing, and expresses merely a preconceived notion.

The Christian life may not be all ease and comfort, but neither is it hard. In the gracious invitation of our Lord He says, "For my yoke is easy, and my burden is light" (Matthew 11:30). As we are yoke-fellows with Christ, what might have been a burden becomes light. John sounds a similar truth by writing, "For this is the love of God, that we keep his commandments: and his commandments are not grievous" (I John 5:3). The precepts of God are not impractical, unpleasant, nor unprofitable. They are in no way grievous or galling. A host of Christians can attest to that fact. The psalmist triumphantly declares, ". . . in thy presence is fullness of joy" (Psalm 16:11). In another place he exults, "Great peace have they which love thy law: and nothing shall offend them" (Psalm 119:165). Does that sound like someone who is bound and living a life of drudgery?

By way of contrast, think of the life that is actually hard and difficult. Solomon was one of the wisest men that ever lived and he testified that "the way of transgressors is hard" (Proverbs 13:15). The sinner, rather than the Christian, has a hard life. The yoke of Christ is easy but the "yoke of my transgressions" (Lamentations 1:14) is one that binds and chafes. It is irritating and brings sorrow, distress, and pain. The drudgery of iniquity and the tyranny of sin are unpleasant indeed, because of a sense of guilt, with its viselike grip and the haunting fear of its consequences. The words of Isaiah graphically describe the sinner's plight. "But the wicked are like the troubled sea, when it cannot rest, whose waters cast up mire and dirt. There is no pleace, saith my God, to the wicked" (Isaiah 57:20-21).

View both of these ways of life and then in all honesty declare which one is the hard life.

4. I TRY TO LIVE BY THE TEN COMMANDMENTS

In this so-called Christian country the people with whom we deal often have a smattering of religious knowledge. They frequently try to use that knowledge to ward off the person who is concerned for their soul. This excuse is a classic example of a misunderstanding and misuse of the Scriptures to obscure the issue. It is amazing how many individuals suppose that, if they try to keep the Ten Commandments, that attempt makes them a Christian.

Although those commandments are a part of the Bible, they are not the givers of life. The Ten Commandments show us our need of a Saviour but they are not our Saviour. Attempting to keep the commandments but shows us our weaknesses and inabilities. Then we are willing to depend upon another, Jesus Christ, for our salvation. "Wherefore the law was our schoolmaster to bring us unto Christ, that we might be justified by faith" (Galatians 3: 24).

If ever anyone attempted to keep the commandments, it was the scribes and Pharisees. They claimed to be more strict in that matter than the disciples (Mark 2:24). Yet these religious leaders were rebuked by Jesus. They rigidly attempted to keep the commandments but still were lost. Jesus plainly said, ". . . except your righteousness shall exceed the righteousness of the scribes and Pharisees, ye shall in no case enter into the kindgom of heaven" (Matthew 5:20).

No one aside from Jesus Christ has ever kept all the commandments at all times. Any honest person must concede he has broken at least one of the ten. The Bible says, then, that he is guilty of all. "For whosoever shall keep the whole law, and yet offend in one point, he is guilty of all" (James 2:10). In the light of that truth, a man has no hope of eternal life if he is depending on his keeping the law to bring about his entrance into heaven.

On one occasion Jesus admonished a man to keep the commandments if he would have life (Matthew 19:16-22). That man replied that he had done so from his youth up. (It is questionable whether or not he had, but Jesus accepted his statement as if it were a fact.) Jesus then told him there were two additional things he must do. The last one was the basic requirement for becoming a Christian, "Come and follow me." The man failed in that and went away sorrowful. Just having kept the commandments was not sufficient to give him eternal life. And our attempts to keep them will not bring us eternal life.

5. GOD IS TOO GOOD TO CONDEMN ME

Many individuals become dangerously complacent by leaning heavily upon an exaggerated sense of the goodness of God. Their wishful thinking does away with the hell of the Bible; they say a loving God would not or could not create a burning hell for men. The truth is that He did not do so. There is only one kind of a hell described in any literature and that is the old-fahioned hell of the Bible. It was "prepared for the devil and his angels" (Matthew 25:41). However, if men are so foolish as to

113

choose the way of Satan, yield themselves to his power, and hobnob with him and his cronies, then they will go to a place prepared for him and never intended for them. They will go there through their own choice rather than by the decree of God. "The Lord is . . . not willing that any should perish, but that all should come to repentance" (II Peter 3:9).

The grim fact is that the person who has not accepted Jesus Christ is already condemned. Instead of hoping that such condemnation will not come in the future, he must realize that it already rests upon him. It is not that God has willed or decreed it but rather that he has chosen it. "He that believeth on him is not condemned: but he that believeth not is condemned already, because he hath not believed in the name of the only begotten Son of God" (John 3:18).

The words "is condemned already" should boldly face any person who hides behind the love of God while rejecting His Son. Again Jesus said, "He that believeth on the Son hath everlasting life: and he that believeth not the Son shall not see life; but the wrath of God abideth on him" (John 3:36). The wrath of God "abideth." The present tense of the verb emphasizes it as a current state rather than a future fear. The person who rejects Christ and twists his thinking to suppose he will not reap the consequences of such rejection is only fooling himself.

6. I AM TOO GREAT A SINNER

Men suppose that there are degrees of sin but in God's sight sin cannot be thus classified. As He sees

114

it, a sinner is a sinner. Hence there is no such thing as a person being too great a sinner and beyond the hope of salvation. If one acknowledges he is a sinner, half the battle is won. Then all he needs to do is throw himself upon the mercy of the Saviour and he will be the possessor of eternal life.

During His earthly ministry, Jesus had difficulty in getting men to understand one basic fact. Even today men fail to grasp that Christ came to save sinners — and that takes in the best and the worst of men. He said, "I am not come to call the righteous, but sinners to repentance" (Matthew 9:13). The apostle Paul wrote, "This is a faithful saying, and worthy of all acceptation, that Christ Jesus came into the world to save sinners; of whom I am chief" (I Timothy 1:15). If His very purpose in coming to the earth and in dying was to save sinners, then do you suppose there is even one sinner who cannot benefit from His finished salvation?

It is hard for us to comprehend that our Lord can and does love sinners. Sometimes in our eagerness to have our children live right we teach them a lie. We say, "If you are good the Lord will love you, and if you aren't, He won't." There is no greater untruth than such a statement. He loves us whether we are good or bad. If that were not so, none of us would be saved. The essence of that truth was expressed by the apostle Paul. "But God commendeth his love toward us, in that, while we were yet sinners, Christ died for us" (Romans 5:8).

The simple statement of Jesus is hard to escape. ". . . him that cometh to me I will in no wise cast out" (John 6:37). No matter how wretched the condition of the sinner, if he can and will come, he may know the joys of eternal life. Any person *can* come to Christ, hence the crux of whether or not he does lies with his will to do so. If he wills to come, then Christ wills to save him. The hope or the lack of hope of the sinner does not lie in the degree of his sin but in his willingness to come to the Saviour.

7. I HAVE COMMITTED THE UNPARDONABLE SIN

There is definitely an unpardonable sin (Matthew 12:31-32; Mark 3:28-29). Jesus termed it blasphemy of the Holy Ghost. However, usually the person who gives this excuse only vaguely knows of the Bible reference to that sin. In almost every instance such a person has not committed the unpardonable sin.

The best approach for a soul winner in dealing with such an excuse is to ask the person, "Just what is the sin that you have committed?" Usually, he will not be able to give a clear answer. That marks it as a weak excuse rather than a reason for not accepting Christ.

Very often a person will suppose that the continual spurning of the Holy Spirit is the unpardonable sin. That idea cannot be substantiated by the Scriptures. The unpardonable sin is a definite act. It involves speaking against the Holy Spirit rather than a rejection of His pleadings. The context of the references to the unpardonable sin suggests that the blasphemy of the Holy Ghost is knowingly attributing to the devil the works of the Holy Spirit.

The person who claims to have committed the unpardonable sin is thinking about something else entirely.

It is unlikely that a person who has blasphemed the Holy Ghost will be the least bit concerned about his soul. He would probably never frequent a church. Even if some do commit that sin, their number would be few. The likelihood of your dealing with a person who is actually guilty of that offense would be remote. If the person cannot tell what the sin is that he has committed or if he assumes that the unpardonable sin is spurning the Holy Spirit, you can be sure he is not hopelessly lost and should assure him of that fact.

8. I WILL BE SAVED AT A LATER TIME

This is perhaps the most common excuse of all. In the apostolic era, Felix heard Paul declare the truth and, even though he trembled with conviction, he said, ". . . when I have a convenient season, I will call for thee" (Acts 24:25). In all generations since then, men have put off accepting Christ until it would be more convenient. That time never comes. With the backing of Isaiah, Paul reminds us of a pertinent truth, ". . . behold, now is the accepted time; behold, now is the day of salvation" (II Corinthians 6:2). There have been more convenient times to accept Christ in the past but all future opportunities will be harder. The human will sets like concrete sets. The oftener a person procrastinates, the more he forms the habit of such action and the more difficult it becomes to break that pattern.

117

There is no assurance that anyone will have another opportunity to be saved. Even if another chance does develop, it will not be more convenient or easier than the present moment. The easiest and best time is now.

Solomon sounds a severe warning when he says, "He, that being often reproved hardeneth his neck, shall suddenly be destroyed, and that without remedy" (Proverbs 29:1). Any lost person should be apprised of such a danger.

9. I AM A MEMBER OF A CHURCH

Strange as it may seem, this excuse is often used as a justification for rejecting Christ. There is nothing wrong with church membership, but it has been geatly abused. It is not a substitute for salvation but should always follow a definite experience with Christ. Generally the person who will express his excuse in this way will be the one who is using church membership as a cover-up. He renders nothing more than lip service to the Lord.

The alert soul winner will explain to such a person that church membership has nothing to do with his salvation. Put in its rightful place, it is fine. Making it a substitute for a born-again experience is folly.

Jesus Himself warned such individuals of the uselessness of an empty profession. "Not every one that saith unto me, Lord, Lord, shall enter into the kingdom of heaven" (Matthew 7:21). This truth should jar the hypocrite or the person who is trying to fool God, and everyone else, by merely joining a church and then forgetting about the responsibilities of such membership. Such a membership is usually kept in moth balls until someone probes about a spiritual experience, and then it is unfurled. It is merely an attempted justification and, hence, only an excuse.

In any competition or conflict of wits, it is wise to anticipate what the other party is going to do or say. Then you are ready to meet his every maneuver and beat him at his own game. A successful soul winner will anticipate reasons, excuses, and answers the prospect will suggest and have an answer waiting for him. If a new excuse pops up (there seldom are new ones) and you can't answer it, then do some digging and be ready with an answer the next time.

As experience develops in dealing with those seeking a loophole, you can adeptly plug the gap and then lead them to a definite knowledge of the Saviour.

ASSIGNMENTS

Become thoroughly conversant with the common excuses offered for not accepting Christ. Memorize one key verse to refute each excuse. Later you can learn all the important verses.

Get some practical experience by having a classmate or someone within your home pose as a prospect and offer some of these excuses. As you refute them you will gain experience.

9. A Classic Example

A GOOD EXAMPLE is the best conveyor of truth. Like an illustration, it serves as a window and casts light upon the subject. Precepts, exhortations, and admonitions can go only so far and then must be clinched with a practical demonstration. A bit of verse says: "I soon can learn to do it if you let me see it done; I can watch your hands in action, but your tongue too fast may run." One example is worth many thousands of words.

The student of personal evangelism can learn much by watching others at work or by hearing actual experiences related. If he is wide awake, he will profit by their mistakes and strengthen his own approach by their proven tactics. The greatest example to us in this realm is that of our Lord Himself. He not only did personal work but also did it successfully and without mistakes. That makes Him the logical one for us to observe as an example of what a soul winner should do and say.

Jesus Christ not only spoke to the multitudes but He also spent much time with individuals. Several instances from the Scriptures could be cited to show His tactics in dealing with one person and the value He placed upon that person and his soul. Perhaps

121

two of the greatest sermons He ever preached were presented, not to huge throngs, but to individuals — Nicodemus and the Samaritan woman. Nicodemus was one who sought out Jesus that he might talk with Him, while the Samaritan woman was one who was sought out by the Lord Himself. From that standpoint, His methods of approaching and dealing with her should serve as an eloquent example for those who would do likewise.

The greater part of the fourth chapter of John's Gospel relates the experience of the Samaritan woman. It could be called, "A Lesson in Personal Work." The soul winner may well read it with the thought of studying the tactics and methods of Jesus as He dealt with a needy soul. With assurance we can pattern our approach and methods after His. In so doing we can be well on our way toward success in winning souls for Christ.

It was necessary that Jesus go through Samaria on His journey from Judea to Galilee (verse 4). A convenient and short route led through Samaria, but that was not why He chose to go that way. (Because of a dislike for the Samaritans, the Jews generally bypassed their area.) It was of divine necessity, rather than for geographical reasons, that He chose that way. There was a soul who needed Him there and that need of hers was the root of the compulsion that directed His steps. It is interesting to note what type of woman this Samaritan was. She could be termed typical of those with whom we are apt to come in contact and the ones we want to win for the Lord. The woman was vile and sinful, and yet she was religious. That may sound contradictory but it accurately describes her. We know she was sinful because of her loose morals. She later acknowledged that fact, although she would not have done so at the time of the initial contact. It is evident that she was religious because, when the subject of religion came up, she was quick to mention her beliefs and those of her people. She did so in an almost belligerent attitude, contending that her religion was more correct than that of the Jews. She was religious, but the only religion she had was that which was inherited from her forefathers. She said, "Our fathers worshipped in this mountain." She was confused in that she thought the important matter is *where* you worship, rather than *how* you do so or *whom* you worship. She could glibly talk about religion, but her confessed loose morals veritably contradicted religious principles. In spite of her supposedly inherited religion and because of her sin, she needed a Saviour. Every day we come into contact with religious sinners whose only claim to religion is through their forefathers. Observing how Christ dealt with this type of person should be of great help to us in dealing with those around us.

Jesus was traveling and came to the outskirts of the city of Sychar. It was noon and very hot. He was rightfully tired and sat down on Jacob's well. Trudging along the path came a woman with a water pot on her head. She was alone, she was a woman, and she was a despised woman in that she was a Samaritan. Should He witness to her or just ignore her? Should He think of His own weariness and just keep quiet or should He consider her need and speak of spiritual matters? She was a total

123

stranger. How should He open the conversation and how could He best present the truth to her? What He did is an eloquent example of what we should do under similar circumstances.

There are six basic facts about the approach and methods of Jesus' dealing with the Samaritan woman that are worthy of note:

1. HIS APPROACH WAS EXCEEDINGLY TACTFUL

Anyone looking for an example of tact will find it in the approach of Christ to this woman. He made a simple request: "Give me to drink." There was no announcement as to who He was nor the ultimate purpose of the conversation. He used no sepulchral tone of a pseudoprophet nor did He give any intimation by mannerisms that He was a man of God. The request was a common one and by asking a favor He put Himself under obligation to her. Because His purpose was not merely to witness, but to win her, He was very careful about His approach.

To the average Western mind the request does seem strange. Why would an able-bodied man ask a woman to walk seventy-five feet down into the well to carry up water just for him? In Bible days it was the occupation of the women to be water carriers. If Jesus had offered to get water for her, it would have been just as impolite as for a man to expect a woman to draw water for him in our day.

In the East, water was and is very scarce and valuable. The giving and receiving of water actually constituted a covenant of hospitality. When He made that request for water, Christ was breaking

124

down four prejudices through that covenant of hospitality. Those prejudices were against the female sex, fallen and immoral women, an alien race, and a heretical religion. By His being a Jew and making that one request, He veritably dispelled those long-standing barriers.

He knew what to say and how to say it. That constitutes tact.

2. HE BEGAN BY TALKING ABOUT NATURAL THINGS

It is most interesting to observe that Jesus did not start the conversation by talking about things religious. He did not say, "Madame, I am a prophet of the Lord and I have come to inquire about the welfare of your soul." That statement would have been very true, but it was not yet time to say it. Neither was that the way it should be said. Actually, He never did say just that, but He made her to know those facts through other means and at a later time.

Contrary to the thinking of some very sincere people, it is not necessary always to speak about spiritual matters right at the first, even when your purpose in the contact is to influence the person for the Lord. Jesus did not do it and yet He was successful in winning this woman. It is not always necessary or wise to buttonhole every person you meet and preach a red-hot sermon to him. Such tactics may cause you to clear your soul of a responsibility but will not aid in the ultimate purpose of winning the person to Christ. When the matter of religion itself finally entered the conversation, it came in such a

125

way as to make the woman accept the truth rather than throw up her guard and repel it.

A logical procedure, and one substantiated by the example of Jesus, is to make every effort first to gain the confidence of the person and then that confidence will give added emphasis to your words. Establishing such confidence may necessitate an unusual approach and may cause you to suffer early censure or criticism. The main point is to know where you are going and maneuver toward that ultimate goal.

The timing of when to speak certain truths is just as important as declaring them.

3. HE STARTED ON COMMON GROUND TO BOTH OF THEM

Jesus exercised a principle of common sense. He sat on a well and was thirsty. Coming toward Him was a woman carrying a water pot. What more logical subject could be used to open a conversation than water? It was something in which both of them were interested and, hence, it was common ground.

An alert personal worker will try to speak of things in which the prospect is interested. At least that is a good conversation starter. If there is an area of mutual interest, that is so much the better. Begin where you have beliefs in common. Start where there is a measure of agreement. That is sound logic and a very wise example that our Lord set for us.

The apostle Paul also struck a common ground with his hearers and then began his sermon from

there. Very often he would stand up in the synagogue and read a portion from the Old Testament
prophets. (The Jews believed the message of the
prophets, and so did the Christians.) Then from
that common area of belief he would preach Christ
to them, and such a presentation resulted in many
converts.

A vastly different method was used by Paul when
he ministered to those of another nationality. Once
he stood on Mars Hill in Athens. He wanted to witness for Christ and preach to the Greeks. Athens
was no place to read from Isaiah or any of the other
prophets. Had He declared that Jesus of Nazareth
fulfilled the prophecies of Isaiah, those Greek stoics
would have said, "Who are Isaiah and Jesus? We
know nothing of them and care less. We have our
own religion." Instead he was alert to find common ground for a beginning to his sermon.

The apostle casually sauntered around looking at
the vast collection of idols in the Parthenon. Finally he said, "You have a fine collection of idols
here." Can you imagine a Christian even looking
at idols, much less making complimentary remarks
about them? Some of his fellow Christians would
have thought he had really compromised with evil.
However, that comment really opened the conversation, and that was his purpose. Those Greeks
beamed with joy for they were proud of their collection of gods. Then he asked a question. "I notice
you have one empty niche. What is the signifi-
cance of that?" Then they made a detailed ex-
planation. They did not want to have an incomplete
collection and so they made one empty niche and

put an inscription over it, TO THE UNKNOWN GOD. Suddenly Paul saw his chance. "That God," said he, "is the very one I have come to tell you about."

While standing amidst idols, and apparently admiring them, Paul actually took his text from a heathen inscription and from it he preached Jesus Christ. It was a case of finding a starting place from the interests of his hearers. He preached the same Jesus as he did in the synagogues but started from a different vantage point.

Your approach will be different to a college president from what it will be to a coal miner. The method of dealing with a cultured Bostonian will vary from that used in approaching a Chinese coolie. A point of interest for a Scottish fisherman will be vastly different from that of an atomic scientist at Los Alamos. An important factor is to start where the interests of the person lie. If you have mutual interests, then start in that area. The example of Jesus says to start on common ground. Straight thinking suggests that we do the same.

4. HE LIKENED ORDINARY WATER TO LIVING WATER

There comes a time to cease talking about natural things and to turn the conversation to things spiritual. Many of the most ordinary objects in life will illustrate spiritual truths and can be used as a steppingstone toward the ultimate goal of all soul winning — a decision for Jesus Christ. An adept soul winner will guide the conversation in anticipation of such a shift of gears. He will be alert to any opportunity to emphasize gospel truths with the help of an object or thought that is already in the mind of the prospect.

Jesus timed it perfectly. They were talking about water. He was interested in water and so was the woman. The subject of water was the one matter they had in common. He did not change the subject abruptly. He went on talking about water but injected a reference to living water of which one could drink and never thirst again. By that simple transition He was no longer talking about something prosaic but a vital spiritual truth. That subject had been broached in such a simple way that they were discussing it almost without the woman's realizing it.

Gifted indeed is the person who can see sermons in stones and who, like Jesus, senses the time to inject a spiritual message into a conversation. He who does not come by it instinctively can develop that trait and let it serve him well in the work of winning men to Christ.

5. HE AWAKENED HER CURIOSITY

Do not underestimate the power of curiosity. When people are curious they will delve into matters that could not otherwise be thrust upon them. A person who seldom nears a church will eagerly come to hear a sermon if the announced topic is one that arouses his curiosity. Such curiosity will prompt the asking of questions and that opens wide the door of opportunity. The personal worker who knows the power of curiosity and lets it work with him, as did Jesus, will find it a secret to success.

The mention of water of which you can drink once and never thirst again just naturally arouses curiosity. It did that for the Samaritan woman. What kind of water is it? From whence does it come? How can I drink of it? Such questions naturally popped into the mind of the woman and crossed the portal of her lips. Anyone else would have been curious and would have asked questions, too. That was a part of the strategic plan of our Lord to bring about that response from her.

It is difficult to deal with a person who is totally unconcerned. You can give him good teaching and admonition; but, if he remains uninterested and merely grunts an assent now and then, your task is not only hard but often in vain. It is futile to try to stuff the truth down the throat of anyone.

It is interesting to see how Jesus aroused this woman's curiosity and in that way got her to asking questions. Any other approach would have made her bristle, lift her head high, and be content with the empty form of religion that she had. Curiosity is a natural trait in human beings. It is more pronounced in some than in others. Plant the seed of curiosity and then let it be your ally to open the mind and heart of the one with whom you are dealing. It will work wonders.

6. HE EVENTUALLY REBUKED HER

Our Lord used a tactful method of rebuking the Samaritan woman but still it was a stern reprimand.

He paraded her past before her, the loose morals, the many husbands, by just asking a simple question. Instead of recoiling, calling Him a meddler, or hurling epithets at Him, she acknowledged her sin and confessed that He must be a man of God to know all those facts. It was almost a miracle that she took it so graciously.

This is a perfect demonstration of the omniscience of Jesus. He knew all about that woman, although He had just met her for the first time. That omniscience belongs to God and not to man. In that, the Saviour has a big advantage over us in our personal work. We have no such knowledge. The woman took that as an indication that He was the Son of God, and it helped her in believing on Him.

If Jesus knew all these facts about this sinful woman when He rebuked her, then He knew them just as well when He first saw her coming along the path. He could have struck a pious pose and intoned, "Woman, I am a prophet of the Lord and you are a sinner. You've lived a profligate life; you have had five husbands and the one you now have is not rightfully yours." Had He made that approach, she would have disregarded Him and would have gone her way, probably telling others that there was a religious fanatic by the well. He knew all about her but waited with the rebuke until the proper time. Those tactics paid off richly. His aim was to win her, not merely to witness to her of the truth. And win her He did by a wise approach and a tactful step-by-step procedure.

Rebukes are proper and must be given but, as with anything else, there is a proper time and place.

Study the example of Jesus and learn through His tactics in dealing with this woman. He approached her tactfully, He talked about ordinary things, He talked about something in which she was interested, He directed the conversation to spiritual truths, He awakened her curiosity and induced a craving within her for that water, and eventually He rebuked her. What nobler example could we ask for?

A personal worker must always resist the temptation to argue. Nothing is ever gained by such action, and much is lost. Very often the prospect will launch off on a conversational tangent and start an argument just to thwart the purpose of God. He doesn't want to face his condition or his need and brings in the argument as a diversionary tactic. More than just the plan of the person, it is the trick of Satan. We are not ignorant of his wiles (II Corinthians 2:11); hence, we wisely avoid any semblance of an argument at any time.

When the conversation between Jesus and the Samaritan woman turned to religion, she immediately set the stage for a good argument. She said, "Our fathers worshipped in this mountain; and ye say, that in Jerusalem is the place where men ought to worship." What kind of an answer did she expect from that? He would likely say, "The Jews are right," and then she would reply, "The Samaritans are right." He would say, "Jerusalem is the place," and she would say, "No, we should worship in this mountain." Each would have stood his ground and when it was over each would have thought himself right. If Jesus had stepped into that snare, there would have been a real hassle and nothing would have been accomplished. Instead, He avoided the argument and said, "The hour cometh, and now is, when the true worshippers shall worship the Father in spirit and in truth." He would not be diverted by an argument but kept directly to the point of winning her. In that action also, Jesus is an example to those of us who would win souls.

It is interesting to note the results of the personal work which Jesus did by Jacob's well. He won one soul but it didn't end there. The Samaritan woman rushed back into the city crying, "Come and see." She didn't wait to go to Bible school or take a course in personal evangelism. She became a missionary to her own people immediately. Many Samaritans thronged out to hear Him because of her testimony. Then they besought Him to stay with them. He did so for two days and many more believed because they heard the truth from His lips.

People who were alienated one from another found the barriers broken down. Jesus had a brief city-wide revival in a most unlikely place — Samaria. Many people became believers. All these things happened because our Lord tactfully and skillfully won one person. That bit of personal work was the key to opening a vast area and bringing salvation to many more souls. The soul of the Samaritan woman was very important, but what happened to her took on greater importance when the salvation of many Samaritans hinged upon whether or not she was won to Christ.

What would have happened if Jesus had been too tired to talk to her? What if He had despised her as other Jews were prone to do? What if He had blustered into the task of witnessing and had caused her to disregard His words?

Here is an example of tact, skill, and wisdom in soul winning. It is also a demonstration of how doors can be opened through winning just one person.

Jesus thought a despised, sinful, but religious, person was important. With that knowledge and His example, we, too, can do what He did and, in the end, cause many to turn to the Lord.

ASSIGNMENT

Envision yourself contacting a total stranger, in a park, at the railroad station, or on the plane. Write down the procedure and response that you would anticipate, basing your approach and tactics on those used by Jesus. Like a game of checkers, a part of the fascination is in anticipating what the other person will do. That part will be lacking, but sketch out how you would approach such a person, and in that way the tactics will become more real to you.

10. Learn by Doing

THERE ARE three basic methods of learning. One is by the process of study, the second by observing the example of others, and the third by doing. All of us have used these three methods whether or not we are fully conscious of them. A baby or small child sees the actions of an adult, or older child, and imitates them. In that way he learns to do things he would not otherwise think about. After we learn to read, we absorb facts and truths from the printed page. The findings of others are passed on to us in that way. All knowledge is accumulative and from one generation to another the truths are handed down in relay race fashion. As we pore over textbooks, our storehouse of knowledge is increased. Perhaps we learn faster and retain more, however, through actually attempting to do things than through the other two methods. We owe more to the school of experience than to any other alma mater.

It is interesting to watch various individuals studying a foreign language. One type studies the textbook diligently, knows each part of speech and the meaning of the words, and can read or understand the language fairly well. In spite of that he cannot speak it. Such a person is the conservative type. He is afraid to venture forth to form his own sentences and express his thoughts in the new tongue. His basic fear is that he will make a mistake and then someone will laugh at him. He expects to learn the language perfectly before he speaks it. The other, more aggressive, type tries his wings in conversation right from the start. He makes some horrible blunders and provokes much laughter, but he recklessly determines to try anyway. The latter type will be speaking the language flawlessly long before the perfectionist even feels he is in a position to try it. A greater part of a foreign language is learned through speaking rather than through studying, although there must be a combination of both.

The person you so admire as a personal witness and winner of souls is no doubt someone who did some blundering when he started, but he ventured forth anyway. He learned personal work by doing personal work. You, too, if you will reach that enviable position, must launch forth even while feeling insecure and inadequate for the task. Isn't it better to make some mistakes in the formative part of your career as a soul winner than to doom all prospects for such success by attempting to be a perfectionist? The person who waits to do soul winning until he can win many will never win any. He who waits until he knows all the answers so that he will never make a mistake has already made the mistake that will make shipwreck of his prospects for being an effective witness for the Lord Jesus Christ.

It is not a matter of whether or not you have the

required knowledge to do personal work or a desire to win souls. It boils down to whether you are willing to launch forth and do what you can and even learn by doing. In spite of your familiarity with the Scriptures, your experience with God, and your eagerness to serve Him, you no doubt feel your sense of inadequacy. None of those factors rank as the most important contribution toward success. The key is a reckless willingness, if necessary, to make mistakes in the beginning and let those mistakes make you an expert in this field in the least possible time. Like the intern in a hospital, you have a background of knowledge but the time has come to learn more by actually coming to grips with practical cases.

On one occasion the Pharisees were very critical of Jesus and accused Him of casting out devils by the power of Beelzebub, a heathen deity who was supposed to have power over evil spirits. They acknowledged that He cast out demons but questioned the power by which He did it. Our Lord answered by asking them a question: ". . . if I by Beelzebub cast out devils, by whom do your children cast them out?" (Matthew 12:27). The truth is that they and their adherents could not and did not cast out devils at all. The Pharisees were critical of how Jesus was doing something that they themselves were not even doing. The question of Jesus stopped their mouths.

A critic once accosted Charles Alexander and caustically said, "I don't like the way you do personal work."

"How do you do it? asked Alexander.

"I guess I don't do much of it," admitted the critic.

"Well," replied Alexander, "I like the way I *do* it better than the way you *don't* do it."

A basic principle of the gospel centers in doing rather than in merely knowing. For some strange reason man has a tendency to be content with knowing, or just giving mental assent to, certain truths. Jesus emphasized the need of doing when He said, "If ye know these things, happy are ye if ye do them" (John 13:17). In his Epistle James made it even stronger, ". . . be ye doers of the word, and not hearers only, deceiving your own selves" (James 1:22). The person who thoroughly knows what he *should* do but *doesn't* do it is hoodwinking himself. He who assumes that just knowing what is right is sufficient is not even thinking straight. It is not enough to know the need and techniques for soul winning. There must be a follow-through to do it.

The process of learning by doing was also taught by our Lord, although it is often overlooked. In speaking of knowing the doctrine of God, He said, "If any man will do his will, he shall know of the doctrine, whether it be of God, or whether I speak of myself" (John 7:17). Notice the emphasis, "If any man will do . . . he shall know." That is another corroboration of the fact that we come to know fully by doing that which needs to be done. You can learn more about soul winning by actually attempting it than by any other means of learning.

Soul winning is the greatest work that has ever been committed to man. It affords a challenge, a responsibility, and a reward. There is no greater sense of satisfaction in an accomplishment than that of leading an individual to the Saviour. In that way you are responsible for his obtaining eternal life. Angels in heaven will rejoice when that is done but they will not be happier than you who have been right in the middle of the eternal transaction. All the descriptions or anticipations of such joys fall short of the actual experience. If there is a need for your friends to be won to Christ, if you know you have a responsibility to witness, if you know how to start, and if you know that such work will provide experiences of a lifetime, then the only logical thing to do is to go to work as a soul winner.

As you launch forth in this great work you will develop certain techniques and methods that will become standbys with you. You will have favorite portions of the Scriptures you will love to quote. You will develop approaches that will be used often. Amidst all of these matters it would be well to develop and make habits of three attitudes. They are not methods but frames of mind. They are, however, just as essential as methods, knowledge, or experience.

1. BE ALERT

This has been dealt with at length in a previous chapter. It cannot be over-emphasized. In athletic contests and in the game of life, it seems as if some people and some teams just get the breaks. Often they make those breaks for themselves. Many times it is alertness that brings them about.

No one can give you a formula for finding an opportunity to witness. Such opportunities come at the most unexpected times and only to those who are alert for them. Practice that attitude of alertness.

2. BE TACTFUL

Tactfulness is not only an art but also an attitude. It is a twofold attitude — toward the gospel and toward the individual that needs its message. The person who uses tact does no harm to the message nor to the person to whom he speaks. He makes the contact in such a way as to bring the two in touch with each other and without giving offense to either one. Tact is an attitude that can and should be developed.

3. BE PATIENT

Because soul winning is not mechanical, and because of the hardness of the human heart, patience is a prime requirement for the soul winner. If results do not immediately follow carefully laid plans, then the witness must await God's time for bringing the person to a decision. Often that is not easy. We see certain truths and cannot understand why others fail to grasp them quickly. We sense the danger of a lost condition and would almost force the prospect to act immediately. There comes a time to stop pressing but to keep praying. We must withstand the inclination to write the prospect off our prayer list if he doesn't decide for Christ the moment we think he should.

The work of winning souls has often been likened

to fishing. Jesus Himself used that analogy when He called us to be fishers of men. A good fisherman must have patience. Anyone can fish when the reel zings the minute the fly hits the water. To find real fishermen, pick out those who are still at it when the fish have ceased to bite. They stay on the job and hope things will be better, while the fair-weather fisherman is at home by the fireplace.

If patience is needed in fishing, it is even more needed by those who deal with wily men who are shy of getting caught on the hook of salvation. Patience is an attitude and is developed rather than inherited. Let it be a part of your tactics in soul winning.

Together we have faced the challenge of personal evangelism. We have sensed the call, the responsibility, and the potential of this great work. The techniques and methods are fresh in our minds and the urge to witness is within us. In spite of all this, it is almost a certainty that you are still keenly aware of your inadequacy. There is a hesitancy in doing what should be done and what you want to do.

A man of God, in days gone by, was in the same situation. God had called Moses to the great task of delivering His people from the bondage of Egypt. In spite of his being concerned for the people and prepared for the task, he began to make excuses. He used five such excuses and God refuted them all. First he declared his own unworthiness by saying, "Who am I, that I should go?" (Exodus 3:11). God answered that by saying, "Certainly I will be with thee." The sufficiency lay with God and not with Moses. His next objection was that the people wouldn't know anything about Jehovah (Exodus 3: 13-14). God answered by giving him an official name to quote as he brought the message. Moses then expressed a worry because of the incredulity of the people (Exodus 4:1-9). He was sure that they wouldn't believe what he had to say. By way of an answer, the Lord worked three miracles and promised also to enable Moses to work such miracles to make the people believe his message. The fourth excuse Moses gave was that he was slow of speech and in no way eloquent (Exodus 4:10-12). He made the mistake others have made in assuming that one must be a fluent speaker to witness for the Lord. The answer of God was pungent indeed. He said, "Who hath made man's mouth? . . . have not I the Lord?" The God who enabled him to speak even haltingly would equip Moses to do what he was called to do. His fifth attempt to evade the call was to pray for someone else to be sent (Exodus 4:13). That wasn't even logical because God had called Moses. After all his protests Moses learned that God knew what He was doing in calling him and it was best to be obedient to the call.

Like Moses, you have been called, conditioned, and prepared to be a soul winner. Look not to yourself, nor to the people, nor to circumstances but look to the One who has called you to His work. Claim as your promise that which was given to Moses in a similar situation. "Now therefore go, and I will be thy mouth, and teach thee what thou shalt say" (Exodus 4:12). Another promise to claim is one that was spoken by our Lord Himself,

142

"For I will give you a mouth and wisdom, which all your adversaries shall not be able to gainsay nor resist" (Luke 21:15).

This book can now be closed. The class period is over. School is out. There is no graduation but this is a time of commencement — in the strictest meaning of the term. It is a time to begin. There will be no diploma with which to decorate your wall. Instead the greatest trophy that will be yours will be the first soul you lead to the Saviour. You have met the qualifications. Now meet the challenge to win men to Christ.

ASSIGNMENTS

Keep reviewing all the memory assignments and expand the memorization of vital Scripture portions as mentioned in these chapters.

Go forth and win souls.